# Also by Leandro Herrero

**Viral Change**

**The Leader with Seven Faces**

new leaders wanted: now hiring!

# new leaders wanted: now hiring!

## 12 kinds of people you must find, seduce, hire and create a job for

# Leandro Herrero

**<meetingminds>**

First published in 2007 by:
**meetingminds**
PO Box 1192, HP9 1YQ, United Kingdom
**www.meetingminds.com**


ISBN Paperback edition:
10 - Digit:          1-905776-02-0
13 - Digit:          978-1-905776-02-3


A CIP catalogue record for this title is available from the British Library

To Thomas and Aisling:

I will build space and time for you
to protect the imagination of your
childhood,
so you can always see the world
with its vast landscape
of possibilities.

So that, in turn,
you can learn to protect yourselves
against all straight-jackets,
black and white,
one-size fits all,
one view,
one way.

I would like to remain simple
as to not to confuse the many
identities I am composed of.

Elias Canetti

# CONTENTS

# [ INTRO ]

# Great players, wrong game

new leaders wanted: now hiring!

# Great players, wrong game

## It's an exciting mess

It's a new world out there. You'll realize this truth if you open the windows of your organization and let in the sun. (You'd be surprised how many companies are run with the windows closed or with some sort of shutters, just to avoid this pernicious flow of sunlight.)

The current organizational climate is very different from the one of just a few years ago. This should be stating the obvious and shouldn't need any explanation. But many of the changes and their impact have come to us at the speed of light - for a great part thanks to technology - compared to other economic, technological and political changes of the past. These days, people sometimes seem to be caught between the realization of the change and the semi-automatic reaction, all at once, all in one afternoon. This speed of changes has left us little time to reflect. The new has taken over in the blink of an eye, erasing the memory of the old almost instantly.

'The world is flat' (and wireless). Globalization - or just regionalization - has changed the rules of the game. You are now competing with everybody else. Your website, online shop, corporate e-brochure and blog are open to the world, not just to those you would like to be the readers. The world is digital, it is an e-world; whether you want it to be or not. Distance has ended. Now, the distance between you and your next-door neighbour is the same as the distance between you in London and somebody in New Zealand. Pace is up. Not only computers run faster, but many companies do as well, as shown by their life cycles. Whether you're an employer or an employee, I'm sure you can add many other things to the list: things that you're now taking for granted as 'the reality'; things you don't question anymore and about which you no longer talk in the future tense. In fact, anybody who says, "*In future, we should do so and so*", is probably referring to something that should have happened yesterday.

This world is also tricking us. Nothing is what it seems or what it used to be. Heathrow airport is not an airport. It is a large shopping mall with external roads where airplanes come and go at regular intervals. The airport's revenues from retail vastly outweigh income from airline traffic, so this is not just a figure of speech. Newspapers are not papers with news, but pages filled with adverts leaving some space for news. Some street newspapers (distributed on the streets or the underground) are free. Eventually all newspapers will be free. It's all different and messy and a bit chaotic. But it has never been more exciting to work in organizations - business or non-profit, public or private - because everything is constantly reinventing itself. You can also add your own list of things that make running your business or working in an organization a very different affair when compared with the past. And this past is also shrinking. Just a few years ago, for example, we used to say that companies could no longer offer lifetime employment as they did with our parents. This statement itself is now already archaic. Nothing is as it used to be, even when we compare it with ourselves working in an organization just a few years go, let alone with our parents.

## Sorry, say again, what game?

Having agreed that this is indeed a different game, the next question is: what kind of new skills and/or 'new people' are needed for this completely different story? Over the last few years, organizations may have done well in preparing their people, developing skills and competencies and building their own pool of 'key talent', as people like to call it these days. The football players are strong, well cared

new leaders wanted! now hiring!

for, well-trained, well-dressed and well paid. One day, they run through the tunnel onto the pitch, with all the new hires in line and all their new gear, the excitement, the energy and the absolute will to win... only to find that the pitch is a basketball court. Great players, wrong game (or great game, wrong players)! This is my two-second diagnosis of many organizations where I am called in to help as an organizational consultant.

An alien just landed from Mars would be forgiven to think that there is an epidemic of blindness in many of these organizations. On one hand, there is an acknowledgement of the 'big changes occurring', but on the other hand, there is little change in the hiring practices, the organizational architecture or the development of people and skills. We carry on looking for the same sort of people, preferably somebody who 'has done it' before somewhere else. 'Somebody with experience'... that is: another great football coach to launch into the basketball court.

In the now ancient re-engineering era, the following joke was often heard. Joe's just been fired after 18 years of service. A manager says to that: "*There goes Joe... just made redundant, 18 years of experience out the window.*" To which the re-engineering consultant replies: "*There goes Joe... just made redundant, one year of experience repeated 18 times.*" Despite many toxic aspects of the re-engineering era, there is some truth to the joke. The only problem is that that assessment could also be applied to Mary and Peter and George who stayed in the organization. The re-engineering movement did not direct people to the basketball court; it only reduced the number of stewards, cleaners and bar attendants on the old football pitch.

## A thousand HR departments can be wrong

Look at the recruitment ads in the personnel sections of major newspapers, including the specialized business ones. Compare them with those of ten or five years ago and spot the difference. Can you? I can't. OK, there are exceptions, but the average company still asks for experience in the same (or similar) industry, for analytical skills and communication skills, for good team players, etc. Most of those adverts also have a computer-generated feel to them. They come with an enormous sense of 'me too'. I don't know whether, as people say, a thousand monkeys can't be wrong, but I do know that a thousand HR departments, recruiting managers or CEOs can definitely be wrong. The only social proof offered by these adverts is the proof of inertia.

As I mentioned before, there is a tremendous contradiction between what we say about how things have changed and the kind of people that we want to have around. These people are mainly a bit like us, maybe with more experience, and above all, they give us a sense of comfort. In my work with organizations, I have wished many times that my client had the courage to bring in completely different people, with skills somewhere in the antipodal region of the current skill set. But this usually proves to be a tough one.

## Reboot, please

Some organizations also seem to be stuck. They are stuck on processes and systems that 'ensure consistency'. They are stuck on traditional people development practices. They are stuck on the same language as years ago, which, incidentally, is pretty much the same language their competitors use. And they are stuck with lots of process junkies on the payroll. In reality, talking about organizational renewal or transformation in some of these companies only means that the oil of the machinery is changed to make sure that the machinery works faster, that the company has new machine-operators and that machine systems have been divided into Machine Business Units. It is going from 'me-too' to a better 'me-too'; benchmarked, above average, a little ahead of competitors or simply 'not too bad'.

But it seems to me that there is only one option when the company and its machine operators are organizationally and mentally stuck. It is similar to when your computer crashes: you have many applications open, they don't want to close down, nothing seems to move, you can't navigate between windows and you have tried control-alt-delete with no effect. The only solution at that point is a little button which - when pressed for three seconds - will conveniently send the whole thing straight to darkness first and then into a new sunrise. It is called 'reboot'. In many cases, we need organizational rebooting, not renewal practices. And you need people with the skills to find the reboot/reset button and the guts to press it.

## Alternative skills

This book does not attempt to re-define leadership or explore all possible leadership skills needed for your organization. It shows you an alternative set of skills and competencies - which I have loosely called 'new kinds of people' - that can generate a greater success for your company. Many of these share overlapping skills or mental models. But I have split them up to focus each of them on a 'desperate new skill'.

You may have noticed in the subtitle of the book that I suggest you should search for these people, seduce them, hire them and give them a job. Yes, the sequence is counterintuitive to normal practice, where you first define the existence of a 'job' (to serve 'a role') and then you launch the quest. This is old football pitch practice. Your desire for these people should be and feel so desperate that you should start looking for them now, even if you don't have 'the headcount'. If you wait to fill in John's post when John has left, you have a high probability of hiring John-II. Your HR department (if you have one), your leaders, your colleagues, your associates and even you must be permanently scouting for these rare species. 'Creating a headcount' for them must become priority number one.

# The 13$^{th}$ type

As for 'seducing', this is the right word, as attracting and convincing are not enough. These people are vital to the new organization; to this new, flat, wireless, fast, ephemeral, no-distance world. With them, you have a chance to navigate it successfully and thrive. It doesn't matter whether you run a big global organization, a division, a medium-sized enterprise or a small one. You need these skills now. You may need them in different doses. If you are lucky enough to have some - or plenty - of these people around, you are in better shape than many others.

These people are also priceless. Make sure that you provide them with the space to breed, even if your own skill set is different and you have won many football matches in the past. In fact, you - Manager, CEO, Head of HR, Chairman of the Board, Section Head, Team Leader or Business Owner - are the 13$^{th}$ type: a leader who understands this messy, crazy environment full of possibilities and whose role it is to seduce those 'new people' and to support them within the organization. You may or may not share some of the characteristics of the other 12, but you will be a 'new leader' in your own right if you accept two things: 1) that these types are far from conventional and 2) that precisely because of this you must take on the challenge and give them a space. Simply put, you may not be like them, but if you have the guts to embrace those skills and those people - some of them unconventional, exceptional, unusual, 'un-manageable' or even scary by your traditional standards - you are a step ahead!

If - as it has been said many times - insanity is to carry on doing the same things and expect different results, it must surely also be to perpetuate the same old skills and competencies and expect a miraculous re-invention of the company. Look around you. The average company is a 'me-too' company, with similar processes and systems and similar skills and competencies. In what should be your desperate quest to get out of the 'me-too' company, you need to switch to contrarian thinking and look at those 12 kinds of people. This is the company you want for your company!

Don't despair too soon if you have difficulty finding them. If you look at the business world, these 12 kinds of people at first seem like a big statistical anomaly, crossing the standard borders of the standard company. But these characters are also in search of a company. You just have to make sure that you are 'that company' where they can act. And this is bound to first challenge your own style of leadership: seducing, hiring and providing the space. Forget the famous 'war on talent'. This is war on elites; the quest for the often counterintuitive set of new skills that can save you from the 'me-too' company trap.

So what happens with 'the old skills'? Well, for starters, you already have loads of them and social cleansing is not a good idea. There are many traditional skills and competencies that history has shown bring good things to the life of the organization. This book doesn't address them. They have become baseline stuff, a pass, a necessity for the wellbeing of the machinery. These twelve new types, however, can come to the rescue and take you to a higher level of possibilities. If you believe that the journey to create wealth is a little bit more complex than a 'continuous increase in quarterly results', then you need to look hard for those different fellow travellers.

## Build the briefing now

At the end of each chapter, I will offer you the gist of a recruitment briefing. It is written very informally by design. In the same spirit and style, I then offer you a 'profile', followed by suggestions of what to do 'in the office' in the meantime, until these people appear one way or another.

Which brings me to the inevitable question of whether these 'kinds of people' or new skills can be home-grown or developed. I have good news and bad news. The good news is that there is no reason why the organization could not practice those skills and learn to act as if there were more of those 12 kinds of people around. The bad news is that a great deal of the skills we all have, started to be developed in kindergarten. Kindergartens, primary schools, secondary schools and even business schools also follow the rule of periodically changing their own oil and benchmarking themselves against the average kindergarten, primary school, secondary school and business school. This means that we are running a self-perpetuating 'me-too' world. Yes, I hope that education will re-shape itself at some point. But it may be a long shot to do your corporate road shows in kindergartens, as it will be a long wait for you to hire that kindergartner when he becomes available. So, in the meantime, I guess it's down to pure hunting.

After that, you need to host them, nurture them and re-create a new skill-base that can deal more effectively with the new challenges. The hope is that, by infecting your organization with truly different ways of thinking and doing, the whole company will gain. In the business organization there is room for a broad spectrum of skills. I am dealing here with the minority: the unconventional and perhaps the life-saving. 12 kinds of people you can't afford not to have around. They won't solve all the problems by themselves, but without them, you are in a more-of-the-same space. The choice is yours.

# [ ONE ]

# Re-constructors of elephants

new leaders wanted: now hiring!

# Re-constructors of elephants

## Analysis: 10 - Synthesis: 0

You wanted 'analytical skills required' in every single recruitment ad you posted in the last twenty years. So now you have an organization full of people with analytical skills. Your people are able to analyze and dissect a project into 'manageable pieces'. Daily life in your organization is pure vivisection. Anatomy is your forte. Any complex-looking thing will be 'analyzed' and cut into components so that your relevant component-experts can evaluate them. Those components are then hosted comfortably on a myriad of PowerPoints. A visiting alien

# analysis

from Greek. *Analysis:* 'a breaking up'. From *analyein* 'unloose'. From *ana-* 'up, throughout' + *lysis* 'a loosening'

# synthesis

from Greek. *Synthesis:* 'composition'. From *syntithenai* 'put together, combine'. From *syn-* 'together' + *tithenai* 'put, place' would be forgiven to think that your organization contains a legion of PhDs in Problem Analysis. In fact, your Problem Analysis is so good that you sometimes wonder if it hasn't become Problem Admiration.

But, to be honest, you like the analysis stuff. You are proud of Joe and Mary because of their 'good analytical skills'. Your people can atomize anything; pulverize, really. Give them any complex situation (i.e., daily business life) and they'll provide electron-size pieces. It's a sign of intelligence, of rigour, of an ability to grasp and understand reality. It shows strong minds, sound judgement and reliability. It gives you comfort and a sense of control. Bullet point dissection equals mission accomplished.

However, it comes with a few problems. For starters, after a while – well into the dissection process – only few people remember what the original problem looked like. You may have heard the story of 'the elephant in the dark room'. A group of men examine an elephant in a dark room. Each of them touches and holds a different part – an ear, the tail, the tusk, a leg – and each of them mistakes the part for the whole. They are all convinced that the ear, the tail, the tusk or the leg is the elephant.

Modern management has updated it to a more surgical version: "*Let's cut this elephant into pieces, otherwise there is no way we can handle this thing*". This has become a regular saying and it may be a familiar stereotype to you. Whenever something slightly complicated is on the table (in other words, all the time) we reach for

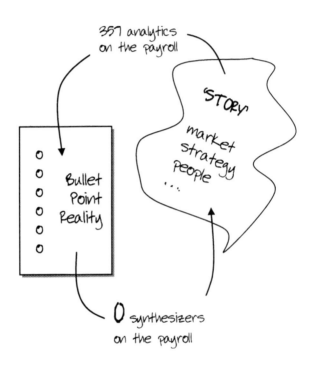

357 analytics
on the payroll

'STORY'

market
strategy
people
. . .

Bullet
Point
Reality

0 synthesizers
on the payroll

Stock:

Legs ... 2000
Ears ... 3500
Tusks ... 700
Elephants ... 0

the scalpel and prepare to understand the elephant one leg at a time. Since you have been hiring managers of great surgical ability, this is not a problem. The elephant - any of your elephants - can be cut into pieces. Your business-salami–slicing machinery is impressive.

## Reverse evolution: an elephant evolves into a thousand bees

A client told me that, in her management team, they used to have loads of elephant legs, tails and body parts on the table, but that they could not recall a time when they had actually apprehended the whole elephant! Vivisection was not only always required, but it was considered 'the ultimate achievement' by the director of their division.

Another client commented that his boss was very strongly against 'broad pictures': another version of the elephant. He maintained that project leaders in the Product Development division should focus totally on their own project, and that any 'bigger picture' was just a distraction. He insisted on giving them 'just in time' information. For example, their attendance at an overall, cross-sectional project review was taboo. He called it focus.

Another example: a group of managers were asked to review a strategic presentation just given by their boss. The familiar ritual started: moving to the syndicate rooms, followed by the 15-minute-ceremony to decide who was the leader and who was going to present back to the main room. "*We were told to summarize our conclusions in five bullet points per flip chart and use only two flip charts*", the most extravert adventured. The Boss' 'Big Idea' was then progressively sliced into a mixture of bits and pieces via brainstorm. Half an hour later, some preliminary bullet points started to emerge. Close to the deadline, all bullet points were in place and the sense of achievement was high in the group. Mission accomplished.

All the above vignettes have something in common: reductionism. One could hardly argue against the beauty of simplicity. However, it has its liabilities. The vivisection director in my client's management team never really understood what an elephant was. In her career, she unfortunately encountered a few of them and could not cope with the stampede. The 'focus-boss' is a real paradox. While preventing project leaders from seeing the more complex 'bigger picture' of a project's interconnections, he goes around praising 'helicopter views' and 'whole pictures' and complaining that not many people have these. The 'report-back-in-bullet-points-boss' has managed to produce precise, simple, pre-digested and applause-inducing information. However, the following day, nobody has a clear recollection of what 'The Big Idea' exactly was.

There is nothing wrong with reductionism. It is one of the essences of philosophy and a human tradition when trying to apprehend a complex reality. Mental activity could be reduced - many people would say - to a mere physiological or biochemical brain process. Social structures and processes could be reduced to relationships between individuals (individualism), as Margaret Thatcher used to remind the world ("*There is no society, only individuals*"). Just as mathematics itself has logic (logicism), almost every discipline has its 'reduced' version. There is no doubt about it: reductionism has paid off, particularly in science for methodological purposes.

## Making sense

However, simplification efforts of any kind have to be balanced by an attempt to apprehend the whole (holism). In recent times, System Thinking and System Theory, Complexity Theory and Chaos Theory, have tried to do the job, but they are still in a different galaxy from business management or organizational life. In one form or another, all of these approaches have in common the premise that the 'pieces' don't make sense without the interaction between them and that there is no point in trying to understand them in isolation.

No matter how precise the analysis of legs and tails can become, the elephant itself is unfortunately not the sum of its anatomical bits and pieces. So, although it's legitimate and certainly practical to 'cut (a problem) into pieces', sooner rather than later, somebody has to put the slices back together again and call an elephant an elephant. And the question is: do you have these people in your organization?

The trouble with elephant-parts-management is that it has an enormous ability to become a core competency in its own right; sometimes even the key competency. So, the trouble with elephant-parts-teams, for example, is that they become progressively skilful in not recognizing elephants – a very dangerous competency. The organization progressively becomes unfit to handle complexity. The ultimate analytical culture goes blind to the whole and literally can't make sense of it.

Similarly, pure 'focus', a skill hyped by modern management, can lead to tunnel vision. No matter how practical 'focus' can be, you will only see a few trees in the forest. The more managers become purely 'focused', the more they will need forest experts.

Modern management education, with notable exceptions, favours reductionism. Simplicity is rewarded, complexity is avoided. The 'bullet-point ethos' rules. We teach, expect and reward managers for their reductionist abilities. We expect 'the net-net', 'the one-page bullet point list', the 'executive summary'. We praise people who can reduce, pre-digest and deliver a 'simple message'.

Could you imagine the alternative, even for a second? "*Well done, John. You have managed to convert those simple issues into a complex structure, adding more elements and enriching the reality. Something that was presented to us as simple has become - thanks to you - complex, interconnected and holistic. Congratulations for your complexity-building capacity.*"

Here are some causes for that unilateral, reductionist, bullet-point-society accepted as the norm:

# 1. Information pollution.

There is so much out there, that we welcome any pre-digestion, filtering and simplification. We are unable to absorb everything. We have simply given up a long time ago and decided that we can no longer distinguish between noise and signal (see next chapter).

In the information/internet-world, we have invented 'portals' that narrow the entry to what we want, or we use 'individualized news', which delivers the latest on pre-selected topics. In any case, we tell 'them' what we want and 'they' filter, promising not to bother us with anything different, but giving us progressively more and more of the same.

Pre-selection and pre-digestion is very appealing, at least on paper. It has the additional, sexy element of making you feel different and unique (my news, my newspapers, my customized search, my Amazon book selection) … until one starts getting saturated with 'individualized' news from different sources leading to a super-customized, super-individualized, unique, tailor-made, for-your-eyes-only, unbearable delivery of personalized pollution. Personalization breeds more personalization, which breeds a kind of world tailored to your own expectations, which will potentially narrow progressively.

## 2. We have also given up on the idea of setting aside time to think and reflect.

Today, thinking and reflecting are activities that only meditation centres and esoteric weekend retreats dare to promote. We are in the 'doing' business ("*We are so busy doing that we have no time for being*"). So if there is 'no time', there is even less time for complexity or any holistic approach. At least bits and pieces are more digestible, we feel. We are also apologetic about the use of time. "*Please skim through my paper and let me know what you think*", we say. Who dares to ask, "*Please spend a lot of time on it and read it in its totality*"? We produce reams full of reading (electronically or old fashioned paper memos) but in these days of organizational life, nobody in his right mind expects anybody to read everything! We produce briefings, memos, debriefings, proposals, position papers and meeting minutes which need to be preceded by an 'executive summary'. On a good day, this summary is what gets read. This 'end-of-time' reinforces any kind of instant knowledge and instant comprehension.

## 3. A 'cut-and-paste' education.

Years ago, my friend's oldest daughter had to write an essay on Israel and did not know where to start. She went onto the Internet (which, of course, is something nobody taught her how to do) and found plenty of pages, lots of pictures and articles, mostly from an Israeli tourism agency. She spent some time downloading, cutting and pasting, and in the end produced a wonderful essay. She got the highest marks. If only she could have read something. She had not. She collated the different pieces into a paper and learnt nothing about Israel (I lie; she retained some sort of holiday information). And not only did she get away with it, she was well rewarded. My friend's daughter definitely had the intellectual capacity to write a good essay on anything. She just did not need to do so. She didn't need to use her judgement.

Is it going to get worse? Peter Drucker was right when he stressed that the manager of the future will be a super-specialized one. Market forces will push harder and harder asking for specific skills. But the more we have super-specialization in management, the more synthesis skills - not the analytical ones job ads are full of - will become precious assets.

Richard Sennett, a well-respected professor of Sociology at the London School of Economics, says that one of the features of 'the new economy' is that people at work, particularly young people, are finding it more and more difficult to know how to get from A to B to C, because in their increasingly specialized jobs they don't need to make the connections anymore. It is as if the boxes of modern work structure (job and role descriptions, specialization, focus) create an obstacle for people to prevent them from establishing those connections, instead of facilitating this. At a recent conference, I suggested to him that the difficulty to establish those connections would still exist, even if for some sort of miracle those constraints were not there …

because, in fact, these people would not know how to do it. Education has little time for learning how to connect the dots. Dot-connecting and sense-making are very weak curriculum skills. If suddenly – I said – the 'new-economy' craved those 'connections of how to get from A to B to C', this might lead to an employee revolution since nobody would know how to do it and everybody would feel cheated. Specialization is like the conundrum of the chicken and the egg: the school system teaches dissection, so we end up with jobs where 'analytical skills are required'.

You need people in the organization with the ability to re-construct elephants from their parts; re-construct strategies from bullet points and re-construct portfolios from individual projects. In looking for leaders, I have not seen any request for synthesis competency that I can remember. But cutting elephants? Yes, quite a lot. Since the bullet-point, cut-and-paste, I-have-no-time (management) education will not produce synthesis people, the challenge for managerial development is first to find those statistically abnormal people and then to nurture their in-house synthesizers.

Your temptation may be to assume that the answer to 'analysis-as-the-only-key-competency' and its sister - 'super-specialization of managers' - is to hire/have/nurture so-called 'generalists'. The problem is that many 'generalists' are in reality super-specialists of superficial knowledge. 'Generalists' are not necessarily good re-constructors of elephants (good synthesizers). They may be, but they also simply may not.

**28**

# Caveat: you think you have solved it by calling in the 'business analysts'

Synthesis is not to create something complex from something that was simple in the first place. Us Southern Europeans are renowned for our 'tendency to prolong things'. The Latin root and written paragraphs tend to be long. We master subordinate sentences and we think that Hemingway's acclaimed short-sentence English - used as an example of good readability - had more to do with his alcohol intake than with beauty and simplicity by design. Amongst my compatriots, we often enjoy an old joke. A Latin parliamentary would say: "*I have a three-point proposal that I am going to summarize in seven*". It always makes for a good joke and is a healthy sign of not taking ourselves too seriously.

In any organization, you will always find people who tend to 'amplify the problem'. These are not re-constructors of elephants. You'll recognize them. If you give them pieces of an elephant, and - assuming that they recognize one and are able to reconstruct it - they would perhaps not end the task there, but they would deliver a complete zoo.

It is interesting how the words 'synthesis' and 'analysis' are misused in business and organizational terms. Analysis comes from the Greek and etymologically means 'a breaking up'. Synthesis, also from Greek, translates as 'composition', 'put together', 'combine'. However, when we call in 'the business analysts', we do so in the hope that they will bring the SO-WHAT after everything is 'analyzed'. We are looking for meaning, for trends, for interpretations. But in the population of business analysts, you get a fair proportion of scalpel people.

Many business analysts are in fact specialist providers of sliced salami, whose expertise is to dissect and 'summarize', not necessarily synthesize. They have analyzed the aquarium and they convert it into fish soup. Their delivery (from the analysis) certainly contains fish but it is slightly difficult to revert back to the aquarium.

You need a plan. You need to treat synthesizers/ re-constructors of elephants as a kind of managerial endangered species. Don't let any of them out if you have them and get some more. If you don't have them, go out and find them.

## Recruitment briefing

Our company has employees with excellent analytical skills. For the past years, we have been able to salami-slice anything that came to us in the form of a challenge. Our key competency is the dissection of elephants.

Over time, we have created a knowledge-based organization singularly skilful in dealing with legs, ears and tusks.

We are looking for new people able to reconstruct an elephant since there is nobody left here who can recognize one.

Remuneration is not a problem.

Previous experience as a business analyst is not necessarily an advantage. We already have loads of them and we are now looking for business synthesizers.

## Profile:

- Sees patterns of things, not its bits and pieces
- Connects the dots
- Is able to reproduce a story from a set of bullet points
- Provides/makes sense
- Can handle complexity without trivializing
- SO-WHAT expertise (We have the SWOT ones)
- Synthesizer
- Sees an elephant when confronted with an elephant

# In the meantime in the office

- Ban executive summaries
- Ban these terms: 'net-net' and 'bottom-line' (Would you believe that there are people using this as a verb, meaning 'to summarize'? *"I don't have time to read your progress report. Can you bottom-line it for me?"*)[1]
- Ban action plans with more than five items
- Ban action plans until somebody explains how the actions are linked and how that linkage connects to the original problem
- Reward people who tackle complexity
- Remember that people who work underground ('focused') can't have helicopter views

---

[1] See: www.theofficelife.com/business-jargon-dictionary-B.html

new leaders wanted: now hiring!

# [ TWO ]

# Signal Spotters

new leaders wanted: now hiring!

# Signal
# spotters

## There is too much out there

The organizational world (business, non-profit, private, public) is characterized by abundance. Abundance of choices. Abundance of actions. In many organizations, the atmosphere is more *busyness* than business. So much to do. So many meetings. So many briefings. So much information to digest. So little time. Large organizations are usually the worst. Their critical mass and 'buying power' generate a self-reinforcing machinery of information. There is never a 'lack of data'. If somebody needs data, he is sure to get it! But the higher the volume of disposable information, the greater the need to distinguish between

# signal

from Latin. *signum*
'signal, sign'. Also, 'used
as a signal, pertaining
to a sign', 'remarkable,
striking, notable'.
*signaler* 'to distinguish'

# noise

from Latin. *noxia*
'hurting, injury, damage'.
Also, 'loud outcry,
clamor, shouting'. Or
'unpleasant situation,
noise, quarrel'. Related
to nausea.

signal (key data that needs serious airtime because it is relevant to a decision, for example, or because it should trigger an action) and noise (background data that contaminates everything and should quickly be filtered out).

Unfortunately, many organizations are run as if judgement is a rare quality and, as a consequence, there is a growing blur between signal and noise. Everything is treated like signal. Many managers seem in need of data to react to, to respond to (action orientation). The last reaction may take over everything else ... until the next reaction.

'Data' comes in all forms and shapes. It is probably abundant in your organization as well. It may be market research data that periodically brings you numbers and statistics on how you are doing compared to your competitors. Perhaps it is internal data from employee satisfaction surveys that tells management about the work climate. It may be a full industry/trade report or simply the constant flow of internet-based news coming to a screen near you.

In my consulting experience, the response to this abundance of 'available data' is often a mirror of the vivisection of elephants described in the previous chapter. In both cases, people play with atomized data. Either they can't make sense of the pieces after the elephant has been cut up or they don't/can't distinguish between the pieces when the pieces are put in front of them. After all, there are so many pieces!

Within a given project, I tend to spend quite a bit of my organizational consulting time *preventing* people from doing things, from 'reacting to data'. For example, an internal employee satisfaction survey may indicate that there are five dimensions in which the company has to improve.  For the sake of example, let's say that they are teamwork, work-life balance, decision making, visibility of leadership and excessive bureaucracy. It seems that, invariably, the temptation is to create five teams which will address each of the themes and create/suggest/implement an action plan of measures to tackle or improve those five dimensions. Very soon, you'll have 50 recommendations … and this is after a few more dozen recommendations were excluded, labelled as 'no priority'. Inevitably, each of those 50 measures (which by now have been 'sponsored' by several senior managers) takes on a life of its own. Suddenly, even if you may have never seen it articulated like this, the 50 'measures' become 'equal'.

They all have a good reason for existence and, as I said before, they were already filtered out by some kind of prioritization. In other words: it's all signal, so it deserves action. The organization that is action-driven, outcomes-driven, implementation-driven and 'flawless execution'-driven is only happy when in action. In that kind of culture, people can no longer distinguish between signal and noise. This kind of organization breeds signal-dyslexic, otherwise hyperactive people who can't 'read' what really matters, can't 'see' what's relevant or not, but 'acts' and 'implements' without any problem. Very busy, kind-of-blind-people… a modern corporate version of the psalmist's: "*They have eyes but they cannot see*".

Judgement is only exercised by a few people: those signal spotters that can pick up the 'aha'. These people are precious and if you are short of them, go and find/seduce them now! They are vital to make some sense of the forest. They understand the context, smell the coffee, see the patterns.

The signals that these people show proficiency in spotting are of a different kind:

# 1. Organizational signals.

Signal spotters are able to understand what is going on in the company, beyond the noise of complaints, whinging and ever growing lists of issues. They possess a finely tuned organizational intelligence (like other people have excellent emotional or social intelligence), spot what matters, 'see' what's valuable and create meaning around that. As an example, many organizations progress towards deterioration in a very slow way, almost invisible to most people. Rules are slowly abandoned, decision-making becomes lax and accountabilities become blurred. If this happened suddenly, it would be dramatic enough for people to recognize it and, hopefully, do something about it. It is almost the best scenario. But if it happens in relative slow motion, real trouble is almost certainly the outcome.

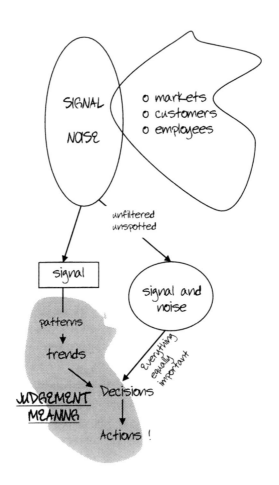

I have called this situation 'broken windows management'[2] because it is reminiscent of the 'broken windows' situation in some neighbourhoods of large cities where graffiti on the wall and broken windows invite more graffiti and more dilapidation. It is permission to litter (in the city) and permission to abandon rules (in the organization). A broken windows culture cannot often be saved by people, other than by those signal spotters and the organizational-intelligent.

You may have heard the story about the 'two ways to boil a frog'. Way one: the frog is thrown into a pan with very hot water. It feels the heat instantly and jumps out before it's too late. Way two: the frog is thrown in a pan with cold water. The heat is then switched on and the water gradually warms up. The frog likes it and stays in. And before it realizes it, it's been boiled. Signal spotters, unlike lazy frogs, are Fahrenheit-sensitive. They feel the heat in the organization and pick up the progression towards boiling. The ones who can't distinguish between organizational signal and noise can't feel the need for change and will get boiled.

## 2. Customer and market signals.

Beyond the paraphernalia of market research and its sister, benchmarking, signal spotters are able to extract trends and interpret data. Signal spotters are more interested in what the meaning is of some data (facts,

---

[2] Herrero, Leandro, 2006, *Viral Change: the alternative to slow, painful and unsuccessful management of change*, meetingminds, UK

feedback, external input) than in the arithmetic of its benchmarking. A decrease in the number of customer complaints that places the company as 'average' according to its industry benchmark, may cause managers to feel relieved. However, signal spotters may see that particular kind of complaint as a significant indicator of poor quality, no matter how low the number is.

Benchmarking is one of the riskiest management input-tools, with more possibilities of increasing a false, blurred space of signal and noise, than of decreasing it. When your company performance is plotted on a multicolour graph and enjoys an 'above average' position, people already celebrate… even though they have failed miserably, because in reality the organization has the ability to excel, not just to be above average. Benchmarking is the business of catching up with a runner who has already won the race. It is rear-view mirror management and the less you practice it, the better.

## 3. Decision making signals.

At any time, your organization may have a wealth of data points with its associated temptation to react, as I mentioned above. Signal spotters tend to reject yet another cry for greater 'availability of data', another wave of surveys and 'feedback', another 1,000 interviews. These are a sign of what I call e-nlightenment fallacy: the myth that availability and transparency of data to all is the basis of good decision making. People have spent an enormous amount of money creating repositories of information, internal portals, intranets and data management systems that allow total availability of real time information.

The assumption is that because of these, they will make better, so-called more informed decisions. The reality is that decision making is largely behavioural and depends on multiple variables, not only on the existence of 'available data'. Lousy decisions can be made with the mother-of-all-data-repositories available to all people; and excellent decisions can be made with only a limited amount of available information. Signal spotters don't get trapped in the e-nlightenment fallacy and are able to pick up the very few topics that matter or the very few data points that should trigger a decision.

# It may or may not be obvious

Signal spotters also even bypass 'the obvious' things because the signals may or may not be in 'the obvious' space. The etymology of 'obvious' is 'being or standing in the way'; that is, something in front of you and in the way, which may mean something you may stumble over!

The following tale has always struck me as a good example of this. Every day, a man guides a caravan of donkeys across a border point. Each donkey carries some bags. The border guard searches the bags looking for things the man may be smuggling. He only finds sand in the bags. This ritual is repeated over and over and the man and his caravan keep crossing the border in both directions, backwards and forwards, routinely. The border guard never finds anything other than sand. Then, the boarder guard retires. One day, he goes back to his old post and sees the man and his caravan. He approaches him and says, "*Look, I know you're a smuggler. I am no longer the authority here, I am retired. So, don't be afraid, please tell me what you have been smuggling all these years.*" To which the man replies: "*Donkeys.*" Signal spotters can spot the donkeys.

There is no better territory than behaviours to illustrate the need to spot what may make the difference and differentiate between a myriad of potential actions. A small set of behaviours has the power to create big change. This is not how we usually think. We think that big issues need big actions and therefore we need lots of new behaviours behind those actions. We think in linear terms. We have strategic reviews delivering a number of strategies, sub-divided into actions, prioritized and often amplified again as actions-within-the-actions. But the organization is not linear. Big changes don't need to be created by a big number of initiatives. A small set of behaviours, clearly reinforced/rewarded, can deal with a significant number of challenges, improvements, fixes or even shaping of a culture. Yes, behaviours create culture, not the other way around. Spotting which behaviours are behind most of the issues and focusing on those behaviours is also a competency of the rare corporate tribe of signal spotters. You need them!

# Recruitment briefing

We are an action-oriented, outcomes-driven bunch of doers; an activity-prone and fundamentally very busy organization (we are fundamentally busy implementing actions).

We acquire and generate such an enormous amount of noise and signal, we can no longer differentiate between them.

Having reached extreme competency in those areas, we are now looking for people who actually don't do things before a judgement has been made.

We are looking for managers who have eyes and can see, have ears and can hear, can exercise judgement and do not necessarily react to every bit of data put in front of them.

Management experience not required.

## Profile:

- Reads/interprets trends (beyond the industry sector)
- Thinks five years ahead
- Shown signs of constraint and doesn't 'react to data'
- Asks, "*What does it mean? What's that telling us?*"
- Asks questions but does not provide the answers before the questions have been agreed upon (actually, people who have all the answers are automatically disqualified for the job)
- Has been found in the corridor saying 'aha!'
- Speaks the language of behaviours vs. the language of processes.

## In the meantime in the office

- Ban another benchmarking study
- Delay another employee satisfaction survey and look for alternatives to find out what's going on
- Look at the organizational thermostat and/or what's happening to your frogs
- Declare, by decree, that the most important management question is "*what IS the question?*"
- Beware of creating beautiful solutions to the wrong noise-generated problems.

new leaders wanted: now hiring!

# [ THREE ]

# Space & time architects

new leaders wanted: now hiring!

# Space & time architects

## The new commodities

Space and time are the new commodities. The bad news is: they have shrunk and you don't own them anymore. You have sold your personal space to a company, an institution, somebody who pays your bills. And you no longer have time either; your Outlook calendar says so. No space, no time. They are somebody else's. These two were your last two assets. Knowledge was taken a while ago. It is now shared everywhere. Skills? Well, that's what shows up when you do things, which is what you are paid for. Money? Earned today, gone tomorrow. It is only yours temporarily.

# space

from Latin. *spatium*
'room, area, distance,
stretch of time'. Also (c.
1300), 'an extent, expanse,
lapse of time'.

# time

Old English. *tima*
'limited space of time'.
From Proto Germanic.
*timon* 'time'. In English,
a single word as 'extent'
and 'point'.

All you really had left were your own personal and psychological space and your time. And now these are gone too. You are bankrupt. Surrender.

If you take a look beyond this apocalyptic picture, you'll see that there are some truths behind it. But space and time are precious assets, indispensable both to you and to the health of the organization. They are intrinsic top level topics for leadership.

## Place

Organizations have places: big offices, small offices, open plan, big headquarters, small headquarters, working from home…. Place is provided. Place is geographical. It can be measured in square meters. We've done that. We have provided these things and architecture has provided us with beautiful examples of spatial solutions to collaboration, teamwork and individual work. Place is not a trivial matter. As Winston Churchill said: "*We shape our buildings and then they shape us.*"[3]

Working in an open plan office, in a cubicle or in a big office with a closed door is far from a simple geometrical matter. It is pure philosophy. It has to do with power and territory. Geometrical power has little to do with pragmatic tailored-to-needs solutions. In many organizations, there is a strict code that regulates office measurements in direct correlation with status. It is assumed, apparently, that a VP needs more oxygen than a Director and that a Director in

---

[3] Churchill, Winston, 1943, Quote from speech to the House of Commons

new leaders wanted! now hiring!

turn needs more than a manager. And suddenly, breathing is a perk. I have seen fierce politics around the size of the office; I'm sure you have too.  Whether place is used as a bonus, as a working area or as a bordered territory, it is all visible and physical.

## Space

Space is psychological. It is the invisible territory where you think, ramble, digest ideas, form judgement, imagine and hear only yourself. A big place doesn't necessarily ensure big space. You can use a big place and have no personal space left. It has been taken over by other people's needs (perhaps even their need of you), priorities, events, activities. But you can have big space in a small place.

## Time

Time was, as I said, your last asset. It was pretty close to your space. When they went, they left together. How we perceive time is a great differentiator between people. Imagine two people who are equally busy. Confronted with something that needs to be done, one says: "*There is not much time for this*", while the other one says, "*We have plenty of time for this.*" The issue is the same, the reality the same; only the perception of time is different.

# Work-life balance and other straightjackets

There is a kind of leader who builds space and time, not only for himself, but also for others. These rare people have the ability to see the need to protect these assets so that they do not become commoditized. They are builders of safe havens. People may think that I may be talking about orchestrated initiatives such as flexi time, go home early on Fridays, no travelling on weekends and many other schemes that have been born mainly from a desire to tackle the so-called 'work-life balance'. These things are very welcome, but they do not constitute a sufficient answer. The reasons are obvious. You may send people home early on Fridays, only for them to plug in their laptops at home and continue to get on with the workload. You may enjoy flexi time, but be overwhelmed by a flood of meetings or activities whilst you are in the office. To ban emails from home in the evening or over the weekend may be a laudable and well-intended measure, but to some people, it may just mean more pressure to compress the same volume of work into 'corporate acceptable times'. As leader of an organization, you may think that you are providing fantastic support to the cause of a good work-life balance but in reality you may just be redesigning the borders and the rules of the game without any other modification to workload, expectations, etc.

True architects of space and time may indeed be advocates of such measures, but will go beyond the visible strategy of "*Work-life balance? Done that*". They are fine builders of other mechanisms:

1. Protection of the psychological, personal space, acknowledging the need for time to think and reflect
2. Encouraging and providing opportunities for formal discussions and debate without the need to 'close the issue' or reach a decision
3. Encouraging and protecting informal conversations via networks of many types without the fear that people may waste their time or 'use it' for non-company issues
4. Encouraging and - dare I say, engineering - face-to-face collaboration, direct talk and less use of digital conversations when they are a simple substitute for the face-to-face

The proof of the pudding is in people feeling that they can control their psychological space and that they are not forcefully evicted from that personal space to live in constant trepidation in the organizational space. These space and time architects are catalytic people enhancing freedom and trust. You need them. It pays off.

Beware: protecting time has a superficial side called 'time management'. There is no doubt that time management is useful, but - like the work-life balance measures above - if this is all you do, you may just be re-creating borders to be able to say that you have a time management programme. Any well-intended, socially responsible, work-life balance friendly, universally imposed measure is no more than a straightjacket of a different colour and size.

## Work climate

Builders (and protectors) of space and time have a great ability to spot the flexibility required to tailor things to people as much as possible and as reasonable as possible. This may eventually be translated into 'work-life balance' measures. They have understood that it is not how much of that the company does, but how much is done in a way that takes into account the diversity between individuals. In doing so, builders of space and time de facto create a great work climate.

Detractors of this are the ones who think that people will abuse this one way or another and that 'one has to put some order to things'. These voices tend to complain that people mis-use what they call 'company time' (meaning, the company possesses the time elapsing between nine and five) and surf the internet or buy groceries online. The statistics show that probably as much as 65% of people would do so at some point during the week. But those who feel less free, more psychologically evicted, will be the ones to take more advantage. If you run the company in paranoid mode, you will get people who will persecute you.

## Recruitment briefing

We are so incredibly busy that everybody is hoping there were more hours in the day. Our Outlook calendars cannot absorb more meetings. Our assistants send electronic meeting requests in the morning and spend the afternoon declining meeting requests sent by other assistants. We have become very proficient at this calendar dance ritual.

We have lost reflection time and psychological space. And all this is happening despite having one of the best work-life balance programmes in the industry. Management is astonished.

We are seeking leaders who can take space and time and build upon them in a way that perhaps we haven't managed to or simply don't know how to. We recognize we need to protect space and time, but flexi time and early Fridays haven't delivered anything visible. Interestingly, people who were exhausted before the flexitime and the

early Fridays, seem even more exhausted
now. We need help.

Time management trainers and providers
of multi-habits, multi-task management,
multi-priority setting stuff (plus
binder or electronic goal-and-vision-
integrated calendars) need not apply. We
already have more than enough of those.

## Profile:

- Readers of philosophy (space & time section)
- Connoisseurs of quality time
- Supporters of free conversation
- Storytellers
- Role models of face-to-face communication
- Protectors of psychological space
- Architects (yes, architects!)

## In the meantime in the office

- Restore freedom of work time if you had it constrained by work-life balance measures
- Stop talking about 'work-life'. It means 'work' or 'life'. It means work is no life … which insults anybody who loves their job.
- Ban the term 'deadline'. Change all the deadlines to lifelines. If you are dead by the time you have achieved something, it's not going to be much joy.
- Ban email to anybody on the same floor or in the same building or in a one km radius.

# [ FOUR ]

# Rightbrainers

new leaders wanted: now hiring!

# Rightbrainers

## The 'split-brain' metaphor

Somewhere between heavy neuroscience and folk psychology, between hard experimental findings on 'how the brain works' and natural observations on the differences between us mortals, dwells the 'split-brain theory'. Here is the summary of all summaries. The brain has two hemispheres: right and left. They work in a complimentary way, but they deal with very different aspects of our mental activity.

The left brain is the home for logic. Speech, reading and writing abilities reside here. It leads the

# create

from Latin. *Creatus, creare* 'to make, produce'. Related to *crescere* 'arise, grow'. From 1678, originally 'imaginative'.

# new

from Latin. *novus*. From Old English. *neowe, niowe, niwe*.

# imagine

from Late Latin. *imaginare* 'to form an image of, represent', 'to form a mental picture to oneself'. Later 'faculty of the mind which forms and manipulates images'.

analytical assessment of facts. It likes facts. Rationality is strong here. Words are words, letters are letters and numbers are numbers: no discussion. So somebody with a dominant left hemisphere - assuming that one side could be more developed, prominent or powerful ... than the other - will show signs of strong so-called analytical skills, will study things in a rational and orderly way and, chances are, will produce lots of bullet-pointed PowerPoints. Order is important for him, which plausibly links with authority. His heart is in the logic of things. I have called these people 'Therefore People'. We've got this, we've done that, we achieved this, we measured that and therefore we go ... there. Problem-solving for leftbrainers follows rules. They are very good at it.

The right brain is the home for intuition and creativity. Images are more important than words. Reasoning on this side tends to be called 'spatial reasoning', with, for example, objects, places and faces playing a big role. Somebody with right-brain dominance would prefer improvisation. He is not hooked on order and total rationality. He may observe and observe. He is more visual. He may generate lots of PowerPoints as well, but with less bullet points and more circles, bubbles, graphs ... (much to the despair of their colleagues who want to translate the bubbles and Venn diagrams into six bullet points). I have called these people 'However People'. We've got this, we've done that, we achieved this, we measured that and therefore we go ...there. However ... (outbreak of horror among the leftbrainers!), we could also do B, explore C and perhaps D.

Let me tell you upfront that the scientific literature on this topic is vast and complex. It shows that there is quite a lot of truth behind the theory, but also that it is contaminated by a lot of half truths and also some rubbish. It is perhaps the natural observation in daily reality that seems to validate this split concept and self-perpetuates the division.

Ever since the 'split-brain' theory became attractive, elegant and popular, people have started throwing more things into the 'left' and 'right' baskets. Because of this, the caricature has grown beyond the real facts. For example, it has been said that men are leftbrainers and women rightbrainers. It has also been said that liberals are rightbrainers and conservatives leftbrainers. The more you polarize, the more you are building a picture of 'bits that seem to fit', creating an even bigger folk-concept. (Incidentally, I am sure that somebody somewhere must have applied logic and decided that therefore women are liberal and men are conservative ... just a guess.)

## The leftbrainer conspiracy theory

You could argue that the polarization itself is a plot by leftbrainers who need to have a clear-cut division between good and bad, black and white, joy and misery! Leftbrainers certainly seem to be in charge of management education. On a bad day, you would be forgiven to think that leftbrainers are part of a conspiracy to take over organizational, business, management and leadership life.

Was the world created in right-brain mode and then invaded by left-brained aliens? If so, they all soon acquired a significant preference for management positions.

Somewhere, a Chief Left-Brain Officer must have created the cut-the-elephant-into-pieces management as seen in chapter one. So I could have made that kind of management part of this chapter. It is its natural habitat. However, it deserved a reference (and a chapter) of its own, given the pervasive nature of the practice. But there is no doubt: the elephant surgeons are leftbrainers.

Serious neuroscience research tells us that - fortunately or unfortunately, depending on which side you're on - the reality of cognitive, brain or mental processes is far more complex than this Manichean theory. And that many processes as we know them today require good simultaneous input from both sides. Fine. I am only using the left/right-brain theory as a metaphor. I accept that things are more complex. But both you and I know that, although a stereotype is a stereotype, well, errr... there are some grounds for the conspiracy theory. We see them in action all the time!

## Left-brain governance

If your company is representative of the average business organization, you will be in an organization largely governed by left-brain rules, led by left-brain people and,

The trouble with management...

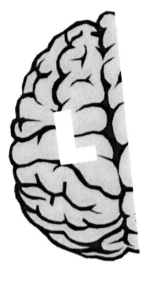

o order
o rational
o logic
o ANALYSIS
o verbal

o intuition
o creativity
o patterns
o drawing
o images

quite frankly, perhaps even proud of it. But the new world and the new organization desperately need more rightbrainers to come to the party. You need new leaders (of teams, of groups, of the company …) who can bring imagination back, who dare to dream of things and who exercise their intuition as well. You need managers of irrationality[4]. You need people playing with ideas and possibilities and you need the risks associated with the fact that you don't have all the facts. You need leaders who can see a spectrum of possibilities, instead of just a 'good one' and a 'bad one'. You need leaders who can work with 35% rational and 65% intuitive probability of success.

## Right-brain vacuum

You need new leaders with the ability to navigate uncertainty and the ability to play with what-if scenarios. You need new leaders who don't have all the answers and, above all, who can imagine the future(s). This is not the standard 'have a vision'. Be careful with the vision thing. Incredibly visionary leaders are dangerous. It may not be managerially correct to say this, but if I were you, I would stay miles away from all of them. They have a clear idea of the future, a clear vision for the company; sometimes as strong and compelling as it is rigid and unmovable. They possess the truth … or so they behave. Extremely visionary leaders have led people to world wars and mass suicides. Extrapolate to your organization and picture the scenario.

---

[4] Herrero, Leandro, 2005, Article: *Managing irrationality* (Can be found and read at www.thechalfontproject.com/ideaslab.htm)

The ability to imagine futures and visualize success and failure in those futures is a precious gift; I suspect from the right side. Most of the traditional and current 'planning systems' are linear. They assume the future as an extrapolation of the present, which is defined by that multi-thousand dollar, commissioned market research study. So, if all things go as planned, we will grow by this much, we'll launch that, we'll expand this way and we'll need lots and lots of new people. The left-brain strategic plan is consistent ('therefore') with the market research data; which in turn is consistent with what customers are saying today; which in turn is consistent with the questions we ask them. It is also market-driven, data driven ... that is, solid stuff.

For left-brain management to work (ensuring consistency, cohesiveness and rational linearity of arguments), a big set of rear-view mirrors is needed. That is why the walkman was not born from leftbrainers since there was no market research data available showing how customers were craving for little boxes stuck to their belts and linked to their brain by a long bi-cephalic 'umbilical cord'. So, for all things linear, left-brain strategic plans should work. OK, good luck with that!

In your company, you need a landscape of imagination, adventure, mystery, play, intuition and re-creation, regardless of whether you are in the business of building engines, developing medicines, producing software or advising on mergers.

Usually, I get two types of reactions at this junction. One: "*This is New Age stuff, Leandro.*" Well, I am all for anything that moves us away from Old Age Management! Two: "*do you mean the stuff you get in advertising agencies, artists, bohemians and other dubious representatives of mankind?*" Well, you can certainly get some dose of 'right brain' in those agencies, but do not assume too much. Some of them are still managed by a leftbrainer.

# From kindergarten to Corporate Normalcy

One of the most fascinating accounts of the organizational world is Gordon Mackenzie's narrative of his life as a creative artist at Hallmark[5]. In a place of supposedly continuous creativity, he found suppression and control by the left-brain management. So, a company dedicated to creativity, yet no different from any other not-so-creative company. He rose to a special status within the company: a sort of 'self-styled corporate holy man with the title of Creative Paradox'. He spent a lot of time fighting the left-brain dominance and protecting first himself and later others from what he calls Corporate Normalcy. The little book is a gem.

MacKenzie reminds us as well that the domestication of the right brain starts pretty early in our

---

[5] MacKenzie, Gordon, 1998, *Orbiting the Giant Hairball: A Corporate Fool's Guide to Surviving with Grace*, Viking

lives. He describes how he was invited to run workshops 'demonstrating his craft' to very young American students, which he did for many years. He used to introduce himself as, "*I am an artist. I'll bet there are other artists here too. Raise your hands, who is an artist?*" The response was always shocking. First grade children used to stand up en masse, jumping with hands raised aiming at touching the ceiling. Of the second grade children, only half a class would raise their hands, very quietly. In the third grade, at best 10 kids out of 30 would raise their hands, all self-consciously. By Grade six, nobody would dare to admit to having an artistic side….

The rationality straightjacket is introduced early in life and develops slowly but surely to make sure that, by day one of their first job, people bring with them a normative view of the world. A view which will bring them promotions and bonuses by cutting some elephants into pieces, following some Standard Operating Procedures, aligning themselves with processes and systems and taking as few risks as possible. Am I being too harsh?

I strongly suggest that you find good rightbrainers, seduce them and offer them a job. Take the risk. Bite the bullet, the same way you bit the bullet points. Hire the creative, intuitive, pattern-recognizing, 'however' type of people and, in the first instance, protect them!

# Recruitment briefing

Please find us some irrational people. We have an orderly, managed, analytically-led, logically thinking organization that is doing well. But we are running out of ideas (we've signed a confidentiality agreement, right?)

We desperately need to think outside of the box and we have tried to do so internally, but people have had difficulties in agreeing the kind of box, the materials of the box, its size, the milestones to develop it and the tendering process to choose box consultants[6].

We suffer from chronic left-brain hypertrophy and we need to discover creativity. You see, our CEO used to call the risky, loose cannon, non-conforming type of guy 'creative'. But since he passed away after an elephant stampede on the executive floor, we now feel freer to ask for those.

---

[6] Modified from a cartoon by Randy Glasbergen, 2001

| **77**

Unusual resumes (for example, hand-written or with pictures of an expedition) welcome.

## Profile:

- Competency in drawing, must still have primary school level
- Risk taking (please demonstrate this by listing all the times you have been fired. The more times you have been fired, the more points you score.)
- Creativity and innovation (we'll give you a blank canvas and we'll see)
- Looks, observes, sees patterns in things
- 'However' thinking
- Brings options, not fully cooked answers
- Fast forward competency: can visualize futures
- Visualizes success and failure in those futures
- Has proven track record of driving linear, rational and predictable people nuts

## In the meantime in the office

- Make Gordon Mackenzie's book compulsory reading
- Bring artists to your project teams
- Give an anthropologist a seat on the Board
- Read Gordon MacKenzie's book again
- Chase the recruiter. It's urgent

# [ FIVE ]

# HCIF Managers

new leaders wanted: now hiring!

# Human Capital Investment Fund Managers

## The investors metaphor

Scenario 1: people are treated as cost. More people means more costs, period. You want to decrease costs … well, you have the units of costs in front of you. In accounting terms, people are simply a painful burden. Headcount is the magic word. In many organizations, the headcount number is *the* number that managers have as a 'possession' (in the UK it's often called 'my establishment').

# talent

from Greek. *talanton* 'balance, weight, sum'. In classical Latin: 'balance, weight, sum of money'. In medieval Latin *talenta, talentum* 'inclination, leaning, will, desire'.
A 'special natural ability, aptitude' - from the parable of the talents in Matt. xxv:14-30

It is synonymous with imperial power (small or big empire). However, 'people as costs' is too managerially incorrect these days….

Scenario 2: people are treated as assets. Who hasn't heard the mantra 'people are our most important assets'? The recognition as assets may be a step up from being treated as a cost, but still people are treated the same as buildings, car parks or money in the bank. These are things that the company possesses, which is exactly what 'our asset' means. Particularly in the re-engineering era, people became the most important *disposable* assets. It generated a vast cynicism in corporate life. That was the fall of the Berlin wall of corporate loyalty. Everything was different afterwards.

Scenario 3: People are neither cost nor assets; they are investors of their own human capital. They invest it in your organization and they expect, as for any investment, a return at the end of a period. Part of that return may come in the form of money, but this is the baseline. The majority of return is expected in the form of increased knowledge, refined or new skills, gained competencies, experience and exposure to sources of learning and development, etc. At the end of a certain period – say at the end of the year - the investor could look at his market value and ask: "*Has my market value increased as a result of my one-year investment here*?" And depending on the answer, they could be willing to continue to invest … or not. But as any investor, they may scan the market and try to find better investment opportunities.

Nobody invests in something for which the return is zero, let alone something where you would lose capital. Human capital in individuals should be exactly the same. Return acceptable? I am staying. Not acceptable? Find a better place. In this 'investors metaphor' scenario[7], the capital (human) is hardly a possession of the company. It is a temporary allocation. The HR department and your own office of CEO and/or senior leader have been transformed into a Human Capital Investment Fund (HCIF). Accordingly, 'management' should look more like HCIF management.

# A place worth investing in

You need people who are experts in HCIF management and whose mentality is not one of assets 'possessed' but one of assets 'invested'. An investment fund manager who doesn't deliver a good return would not be worth his title and role. Similarly, HCIF Managers who can't prove that they have grown human capital assets in the organization would not be doing their job. Investors (you and me) would leave that fund and search for a better performing one.

HCIF Managers are not confined to the HR department, but are scattered all over the place in positions of management and leadership. In fact, the HR department is now rather an administrative centre for the HCIF, no more, no less. It has the key role of supporting the HCIF

---

[7] Davenport, Thomas O., 1999, *Human Capital: What it is and Why People Invest It*, Jossey-Bass, San Francisco

Managers and of developing those skills in others. It is a school of and for investors, although the majority of investors learn investing by investing.

In this useful metaphor/scenario, the individual - like an investor - has significant power. Mechanisms of trust (in you managing my assets) play a key role. By this I mean environmental conditions in the organization. A place worth working at, becomes a place worth investing in. Hiring people is seducing them into a compelling story of investment. As in any investment, you'll find several forms of capital floating around. In the organization - as well as the money capital and the fixed assets of plants and machinery, if you have those - you'll find:

- Human Capital: the pool of talent that is investing in your company at any given point.
- Social Capital: the pool of relationships (internal and external, quality and quantity) that the investors bring and develop
- Architectural Capital: how investors work together, how effectively they team up or network, how they are organized and function

The sum of all those forms of capital constitute the organization's I.Q: an index of how well it's doing in attracting investors, retaining them and developing others into better investors. Since it is more than 'intelligence' in the intellectual and talent sense, we should call it I+E+S Q.

## Non-monetary organizational asset map

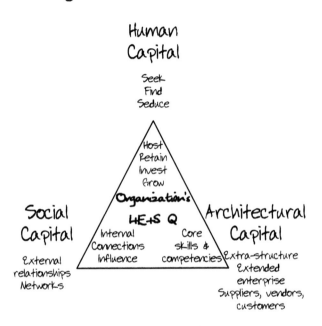

Human Capital

Seek
Find
Seduce

Host
Retain
Invest
Grow

Organization's

HE+S Q

Social Capital

External relationships
Networks

Internal Connections
Influence

Core skills & competencies

Architectural Capital

Extra-structure
Extended enterprise
Suppliers, vendors, customers

The organization's IQ is better defined in a broader concept that not only includes 'intelligence' (IQ), but also emotional competencies (EQ) and social/associability skills (SQ)

That is, talent plus emotional intelligence (EI) and social intelligence (SI). They are interconnected. EI deals with the ability to integrate and use emotions in the management of the fund. SI deals with the capacity to understand how the dynamics of the fund work in terms of relationships and work climate.

It is this kind of capital (or capitals) that - when applied to the organization's mission - delivers the goods, creates the wealth or in summary, makes the company work. Of course, the company has other investors of the traditional kind, who put money in instead of human capital. They are not the employees but the stakeholders. But it is impossible to satisfy the money-investors without giving the human-capital-investors a good return. Temporarily, the former may get away with good returns without growing the human capital, but this is not a good long-term investment for them. It is in the money-investors' best interest that the human-capital-investors get a good return. Not necessarily for any altruistic or humanistic reasons of 'respect', but as the only guarantee that the company will deliver what it is supposed to deliver.

In previous scenarios (people acknowledged as assets) and in many cases, people are treated with respect, rewarded with a handsome salary/bonus and offered lots of training. But they don't quite ever get to be on equal footing with the external money-investors, because the standard definition of a public company's reason for existence is 'to maximize shareholder value'. In private companies, this will be the ownership and in non-profit companies it will be the provision of services, satisfaction of stakeholders and enough money to pay salaries.

## Employees first (no moral attachment necessary)

In some companies - though probably not the norm these days - there is a special 'human respect', which, particularly in the past, used to stem from some sort of spiritual context, e.g. Christian values. In those cases, employees may have been well taken care off. And in some heroic cases, redundancies were even avoided in times of war or economic depression. In those cases, as in other milder versions seen today, the employee is 'upgraded' for ethical reasons. The employee's equal footing to other players is by design, driven by a value base that induces it. Again, even in those cases, the equal footing is *granted*, it doesn't come naturally.

In standard Western organizational management, we constantly cross swords with the three musketeers: customers, stake/share-holders and employees. If you ask anybody in a management position who comes first, chances are they'll give you the politically correct answer that they are all equal, because the company can't function without satisfying all of them. If you insist hard enough, you'll find that some are more equal than others. Statistically, when you dig deep enough (and very often even without the digging), shareholders come first. Isn't it a paradox that I don't know anybody who wakes up in the morning looking forward to maximizing shareholder value during the day…?

Very few companies have the guts to put employees first. One I know is Southwest Airlines in the USA which doesn't hesitate to say, "*Customer, you come second*". This company has transformed its industry by inventing the low-cost airlines. It also outperforms markets and expectations systematically.

You need leaders who are HCIF Managers; who really believe in and live the 'investors metaphor' and who are good at spotting talent ('connoisseurs' of talent). They are also good at creating the conditions to host and grow the investment, doing so not just on ethical grounds, but with clear organizational goals.

## Believing in the investment

Most investors believe in their investments; that's why they bet on them. It sounds almost silly to state this, but when it comes to people, many 'people managers' behave as if they are dealing with the enemy. Entire HR and non-HR departments have an unwritten motto: 'hell is other people[8]'. This is completely opposite to the way Benjamin Zander - the conductor of the Boston Philharmonic and an acclaimed and prestigious conservatory teacher, who has ventured into the leadership arena - treats people. At the beginning of the year, he gives students an 'A', and at the

---

[8] Sartre, Jean-Paul, 1944, *Huis Clos (No Exit)*

end, he asks them to write a document explaining how they deserved that 'A'. Many are astonished at the beginning, knowing that they are not 'A material'; maybe they even came to the conservatory with low credentials. Conventional wisdom would say that it is not a good idea to presume an 'A' because - and here is our 'concept of man' – people will abuse it, will do nothing and will lose interest having obtained the highest qualification already. Instead, Zander's pupils thrive and work during the year to justify the 'A' that has already been given to them. In one of his unique 'leadership performances', Zander once said: "*you won't believe how good an orchestra of 'A's sounds!*" This figure of speech has stayed with me ever since.

The first step in believing in your HCIF management is knowing and believing that the HC that constitutes your IF is of quality; that it's something that is going to work and that you are going to nurture and grow. You don't invest in hell. If people are 'a pain', managing the IF will be painful, most likely even miserable. If you have a fund of 'Cs' that need to prove they can become 'As', you convert the journey into the road to hell. And you won't believe how miserable an orchestra of C's sounds.

## The war on talent, HCIFM style

A few years ago, some McKinsey consultants invented the term 'the war on talent'. The term gained great popularity and is still widely used. But the war on talent distracted people from the hot issue of how to host/retain

**92**

talent; both the talent you already have or the talent you bring home from your crusades. HCIF Managers are by definition working as external Knights Templar in the crusades and as internal organizers of the conditions for human capital growth. You need to have those people around. And your challenge is not only going to be spotting them and seducing them, but making sure that they really are what they are supposed to be. By that I mean that speaking a 'people language' is no guarantee of being a good HCIF Manager. I am afraid you'll have to find some proof that they can grow what they invest.

Incidentally, all this applies to you as well. If you are in the business of finding HCIF Managers, if you lead the organization, then you are the Chief HCIF Manager.

# Recruitment briefing

The most important assets of our organization are our people, but we have just figured out that (a) another 3,000 competitors say the same and (b) we lost a bit of credibility here due to our last 25% reduction in workforce. We are looking for new leaders at all levels of the organization. Leaders who can spot talent and develop it in such a way that the talent-holder doesn't ever want to go anywhere else. We recognize that the 'ever' is a bit countercultural, but that's just us.

We are serious about growing our collective IQ because in the long term (but also in the short and medium term) this is the only thing that will distinguish us.

Please bring proof of your success as an investor. HR (and training) backgrounds welcome, but only with proof that you were really heard by your management and that you actually made a difference.

## Profile:

- Investment background
- Venture capital background
- Creates conditions for IQ growth
- People enhancers
- Spot talent
- Spot people who develop relationships and use them
- Expert in organizational climate change
- Followers of the philosophy of 'You-got-an-A-explain-why'.

# In the meantime in the office

- Convert everybody into a HCIF manager. Learn about investing (yes, investing itself)
- Have your 'war on talent' converted into an active 'war on ideas'. Find those people with new ideas!
- Be prepared to spot/seduce talent in whatever form or description you want to use. But this means accepting and embracing diversity.
- Adapt your procedures so that the right talent can navigate your company without unnecessary constraints.
- Implement vehicles for human capital growth such as job shadowing (and if you have job sharing schemes, make sure that they do not become simple task sharing).

new leaders wanted: now hiring!

# [ SIX ]

## Lead(brok)ers

new leaders wanted: now hiring!

# Lead(brok)ers

## Organizational brokers

A broker in the original sense of the word is somebody who buys and sells goods or assets for others. But in a broader sense, a broker is also somebody who acts as an intermediary, a facilitator, a mediator, a negotiator or an agent. It is somebody who organizes, orchestrates and facilitates plans going live. Inside modern organizations, there is a huge interdependency between people, teams and divisions, but this interdependency also exists between the company and other firms, suppliers, customers (and any permutation of any of the above). Brokerage is crucial. A Senior Manager today must be a Senior Broker. Being a manager is no longer about dictation, command and control or about beautifully crafted mission statements, leaving the

new leaders wanted: now hiring!

# lead

Old English. *lædan*
'cause to go with one,
lead', 'to guide'. Also 'to
travel'. Leadership first
described in 1821.

# broker

From Anglo-Normand.
*brocour* 'small trader'.
And from Anglo-French
*abrokur* 'retailer of
wine, tapster'. Also from
*broche* 'pointed tool',
'wine dealer'. Later
'retailer, middleman,
agent'.

'implementation' to the troops. The troops these days can't function without reference to other troops, starting with the ones that are part of the same company!

Let's look at an example. The enterprise has been re-designed and cut into pieces called 'Business Units'. If this is going to work, it will not only need several 'structures' (the Head of the new Business Unit, plus management, plus the rest of the cast) but also a 'brokerage' structure co-ordinating relationships between them. Otherwise, each of the newly appointed sub-CEOs will go full steam ahead, only concerned by what is good for his/her own unit.

One of the common complaints in the implementation of a 'Business Unit Model' is that 'they (people) don't talk to each other anymore'; or in other words, that the common opportunities and the leverage that the 'single entity' used to provide are now missing. The complaint is usually well-founded. Most of the time, this is because there is no brokerage structure in place. The new organization-charts look slimmer, sexier and more fashionable, but nobody actually has a clue as to how to cross-function in this completely different business model.

You desperately need brokerage skills mixed with leadership skills. Lead(brok)ers need to come to the rescue and must be incorporated into the fabric of a modern enterprise. In the multiple level, interdependent network society (external networks with suppliers, customers and other stakeholders; internal networks of teams, divisions,

'Business Units' and self-contained P&L entities) we need them big time.

## Brokering in the commons

We may be falling into the usual trap of management insanity here, pretending that the simple establishment of a new 'function' (of lead(brok)er) will automatically do the trick. For the brokerage to be successful, the 'function' sometimes has to be performed at a senior level. In the example above, entire Vice-President offices should be no more than a lean operation with the sole function of making sure that the Business Units talk to each other, that they do not totally compete for the same clients and that they are all making the most of their 'sovereignty' but without the associated cost.

Autonomous Business Units, split R&D and parts of the firm competing for limited resources need brokers who understand, can navigate and perform in *The Tragedy of the Commons*[9]. In this parable, herdsmen use the free pastures of the village commons to feed their animals. The more animals they bring in, the more they can sell. When all the herdsmen think the same way, the tragedy occurs: the commons are overgrazed and destroyed and there is nothing left for anybody. In a broad sense, *The Tragedy of the Commons* means that looking at the world through your own single lenses only - disregarding the world of others - leads to an ugly world for everybody.

---

[9] Hardin, Garrett, 1968, *Science* 162, 1243-1248

In management terms, if all the 'independents' within the firm (the herdsmen) are left to their own devices they will seek the maximum return for their Business Units, not caring much for their fellow leaders. Tragedy occurs when they do not talk to each other to ensure that whatever they do, there is going to be enough pasture (budget, client relationship, priorities….) for everybody. They need a brokerage system that first confronts them with the potential 'tragedy' and then also facilitates the dialogue and the leverage. Independent units need good lead(brok)ers.

Those needed lead(brok)ers must have the skills and capabilities to be brokers *and* to lead from that perspective. They must know how to do what the dictionary says: facilitate, negotiate, orchestrate and mediate. They are leverage-spotters and opportunity-seekers, without necessarily being in charge of any of the 'Units' and with respect for their independence. They are the guardians of the commons, without owning a single sheep[10]. To understand how they exercise lead(brok)ership we need to look at these five dimensions:

# 1. Bridging, building, gluing

Above all, lead(brok)ers are masters of relationships. It is unlikely that any good lead(brok)er is not social-intelligent. The way they build bridges and 'integrate' people is usually horizontal: across groups or divisions,

---

[10] I have developed this angle of lead(brok)ership in my book *The Leader with Seven Faces* (meetingminds, 2006)

across interests. You may have come across those individuals who seem to have a tremendous ability to glue things, to put things together, to make sure that Mary and John are talking, with or without them present. They represent an extremely valuable asset and, incidentally, they may or may not be in senior management.

I know of people in 'support functions', such as HR or Organizational Development, who spend a fair amount of their time building bridges between other people, sometimes at a very senior level. I also know of people at high levels doing the same. These people are gems. And if you can't identify them in your organization, I suggest you search hard for this 21$^{st}$ century organizational skill!

## 2. Clearing the way

Another aspect of lead(brok)ership is the tearing down of barriers so people can actually do their jobs. In many organizations, success seems to happen despite their processes and systems, not because of them. Spotting and eliminating barriers is a precious skill, very often best exercised in the background and without much noise.

In many cases, a good lead(brok)er has the guts to confront a more or less senior person: "*Harry, we have a problem and we are glad to say we found it: it's you!*" I leave you to judge if any modification of the statement is needed, but the reality is that, in many cases, bottlenecks are at the top, not in the usual target mother-of-all-scapegoats: middle management. Frankly, the word bottleneck says it all: it is at the neck.

In many cases, getting out of the way should be high priority for management. The fear of losing control is one well established in traditional management. Control itself – with its associated paraphernalia of 'processes' and 'systems - is the barrier. Lead(brok)ers get themselves out of the way or facilitate others to do the same.

## 3. (Back)stage management

Most of the good lead(brok)ership stuff is fairly invisible. Lead(brok)ers are stage managers without the visibility of the Almighty Project Manager. Some project managers have, by the time they get appointed, probably already gained an extra word on their business card, becoming Global Project Manager, as part of a Global Function that sits in the Global Structure. The trouble with Global Project Leaders and Managers is that they have reached the ceiling of earthly promotion. After Global, they can only become Pan-Galactic, with considerable consequences for the travel budget.

Common features of good lead(brok)ers are being more or less invisible, certainly not prominent, and capable of backstage and stage-management, instead of 'project management'. That is why having an ego the size of a cathedral is incompatible with being a lead(brok)er. I have always found it interesting that backstage brokerage is considered 'normal', acceptable and almost predictable in a

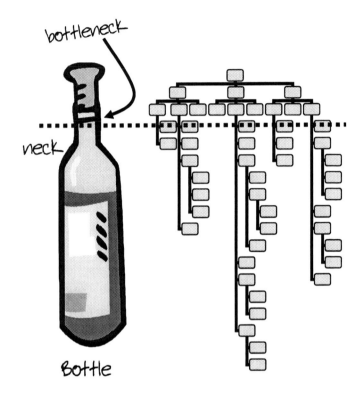

**Lead(brok)ers:**
- Leader of the Commons
- Bridge builder
- Barrier clearer
- Facilitator
- Stage manager
- Noise pollution policeman
- Deal maker

field such as politics, but when it comes to organizations we assume that 'that role' can only be played by visible, often high ranking people.

Backstage political brokerage has often occurred between political factions that officially don't talk to each other. It is an assumed rule of the game that invisible (to the external world) communication channels need to be open constantly, even when Big Political Leaders at the top declare that there are no communications. I can't think of a better recent example than the Irish conflict, where some unknown religious figures played a brokerage role between the UK, the Irish government and the paramilitary. I am told that some of these people - who have now become unemployed - have been 'exported' to other murky areas such as the Spanish Basque country. That makes sense to me, because backstage, invisible brokerage is a precious leadership asset.

## 4. Effectively distributed leadership

The distributed leadership model implies that leadership can be found at all levels of the organization and not only in the boxes at the higher levels of the organization chart. Mutual influence, modelling behaviours, endorsing actions, building support, 'influence without authority' in all its forms, all constitute an engine of 'practicing leadership'. In this model, there is little need for theoretical workshops and grandiose lectures on leadership. Modelling this leadership *is* leadership. Period. Lead(brok)ers are a fantastic role model because very often they open people's minds as to how - in practical terms - to build those bridges, to get people to talk, to prepare the stage for negotiation and ultimately to exercise enormous influence. The best deal-making is silent. Many managers can learn this from active lead(brok)ers in the field, and, if this is the case, you have de facto a free leadership development programme.

## 5. Managing the organizational decibels

The average company manager spends 90% of his/her time managing inwards and 10% managing the external customer side. OK, if you think this is an exaggeration, be grateful, you are lucky. In this inwards looking management-of-the-inevitable, an enormous amount of noise is generated constantly. What some people said or didn't say; what some groups will or won't support; whether 'they' think that you have a problem or not; what's happening or not happening; that marketing doesn't really like what they see in R&D; that R&D doesn't trust marketing; that we are going to be reorganized; that we are definitely not going to be reorganized ... that the sky is falling. The noise pollution is high and decibels go up with the next chain of people (teams, groups) tuning in. In such a noisy environment, you can't hear the real conversation. Lead(brok)ers have the great ability to decrease the noise, to calm things down, to quietly find the assumed source and put things in perspective. Most of the good lead(brok)ers I know always spend some time turning down the volume.

If you don't have these people, go and find them. A few of them can transform the organization in multiple ways. They are another endangered species that need special treatment.

## Recruitment briefing

Our last reorganization into Business Units and the split of the business into five 'autonomous' groups has provided us with significant focus and customer orientation. It has also created five new silos competing for ideas, resources and corporate airtime. We were told by a Big Consulting Group that internal competition was healthy, but nobody taught us about internal collaboration.

We are seeking to recruit people who can build bridges and orchestrate backstage collaboration across the board, at several levels of the organization, without being the Big Budget Holders. These people should be able to manage conflict from the background, bringing people together.

Management experience not necessary, but it is important to know what deals he/she obtained from kindergarten onwards.

## Profile:

- Builds support as a matter of principal
- Facilitation
- Strong role modelling
- Catalytic
- Horizontal connectedness (not hooked on top-down philosophy)
- Broker
- Deal maker
- Ability to tap into any source of good human capital and to make sure that it is shared
- Backstage manager
- 'Invisible hand'

# In the meantime in the office

- Establish collaboration as key competency, above competition (it may take you a little while)
- Make *The Tragedy of the Commons*, compulsory reading for everyone from the post room to the executive floor
- Don't respond to noise
- Establish public prizes for spotting barriers and suggesting how to remove them
- If you are in management, think of one situation/project/activity where you can make the best possible contribution by disappearing from the map

# [ SEVEN ]

# Riders of the network

new leaders wanted: now hiring!

# Riders of
# the network

## We live in a teamocracy

The average company is organized in teams. Think of something to be done and somebody will shout: "*Let's have a team*!" We have all sorts of teams: functional teams, cross-functional teams, management teams, project teams, user teams, HR teams, leadership teams, tiger teams, high performance teams, dysfunctional teams, norming teams, mature teams, etc. We have consultants, books, conferences and training programmes on team effectiveness, team formation, team alignment and team progression. We have team members (core team members

# network

1560, from *net* (n.) + *work*
'net-like arrangement of
threads, wires, etc.' 1839,
'any complex,
interlocking system'
(originally related to
transport by rivers,
canals and railways).
1914, 'broadcasting
system of multiple
transmitters'. 1947,
'interconnected group of
people'. The verb in ref.
to computers dates from
1972.

and extended team members) and team leaders. We have anthropomorphized the teams and ascribed to them mental capacity expressed in ways such as: the team has decided, the team has reached, the team agrees, the team recommends. The team rules the waves.

We ask the teams to focus, to be cohesive, to have clear goals and objectives, to concentrate on their mission and to not get distracted. We expect them to discuss, to get information and digest it, to establish priorities, to manage some resources, to meet milestones, to be on target and on budget.

Above all, we take for granted that 'the team will meet'. And oh boy, does it meet. The team meeting is the climax of the teamocracy[11]. It is a cyclical phenomenon as predictable as the sun rising and setting. The early warning signals of an approaching team meeting are a frenetic activity around something called 'the agenda' which needs to be populated with agenda items. This fever announces the arrival of the peak of the cycle. Then, the meeting takes place. On average, people feel good because decisions have been made and 'issues have been closed'. The crescendo has been reached during the meeting and now everybody slides down the energy curve. And the energy eventually seems to fade or is at least no longer noticeable. After a silent period, a new early warning system kicks in and new agenda items are sought. The cycle starts again.

---

[11] Herrero, Leandro, *Competing on Collaboration: Teamocracy and its discontents* (to be published by meetingminds)

One of the most awful illnesses of the teamocracy is the tacit assumption that 'team meeting' equals 'team'. We have equalized the act of meeting up with the nature of the team itself (association of individuals). People use expressions such as 'bring this to the team' or 'needs to be solved at the team', meaning in reality 'bring this to the meeting' or 'needs to be solved at the meeting'.

It is only normal that - having accepted the idea that 'a team' is the standard and default way for human collaboration in the organization - we spend a lot of time designing the artefact 'team' and making sure that we (management?) control the borders, the constitution and the governance. Teams constitute collaborative spaces by design. It is collaboration by decree: "*You will collaborate, John, you will (need to) be a team player. You'll play by the rules.*"

# The innovation quest(ion)

Carried away by the excitement of these collaborative platforms and their pristine borders, we then start expecting even more of the teams. Many people in the company say that teams are the engine of innovation. And the expected process for innovation is outlined: "*OK, this is your constituency, here are the rules, this is what you do and don't do. Here is the money, Peter is the leader, you are in norming to storming phase. Have your monthly meetings, have an agenda, produce minutes, don't deviate, focus, focus, focus. There you go. Now, innovate.*"

Innovation requires, amongst other things, the ability to seek unpredictable answers[12]. With the whole outlined script - including a designed constituency, designed rules, this is what you do and don't do, fixed money, appointed leader, predetermined meetings, standard agenda, War-and-Peace sized minutes, and focus, focus, focus - unpredictability is hardly a characteristic of the team. If you are seeking unpredictable answers from team mates Bob, Peter, Carole and Alice with whom you work every day or have some sort of close team relationship, chances are … you won't get them.

Innovation needs connections with people you don't or hardly know. This is what sociologists call 'weak ties'[13]. Teams breed strong ties. Whilst you may need teams as part of your operational machinery, you also need loose networks of people ('belonging' to different places/teams) talking to each other, to tap into sources of human capital which may bring something new to the party. Most of those networks are invisible. You won't find them on the organization chart.

## Hosting conversations

As a rule of thumb, only about one quarter of the good stuff happens in the designed, controlled, bordered

---

[12] Herrero, Leandro, 2005, Article: *The Innovation Mindset* (Can be found and read at www.thechalfontproject.com/ideaslab.htm)
[13] Granovetter, Mark, 1973, The Strength of Weak Ties, *American Journal of Sociology*, Vol. 78, Issue 9, pp. 1360-1380.

and structured part of the organization that hosts teams, committees, task forces and any other collaboration-by-design spaces. The other three quarters occur in the mostly invisible, loose, un-structured social network of people having 'conversations" outside the formal structures of teams and committees. We have based our whole management theory and practice on only 25% of the space!

Many years ago, some clever people made the observation that the real value of big meetings and conferences was in the conversations taking place during the coffee breaks. So they invented the 'open space' concept of meetings, where people create their own agendas and spaces[14]. If you want a truly innovative company, able to tap into everybody's brains and hearts, construct the company as a very, very long coffee break.

## Citizenship

The old view of the organization is something close to the old concept of a medieval city, where citizenship was defined by inhabiting and dwelling within an area defined by the walls of the castle. The new view of the organization is similar to the concept of a modern city, where citizenship is defined by moving around a network of communications (in multiple directions with multiple connections) with very permeable borders, if any. Nodes in this network are both destination and point of departure at the same time.

---

[14] Owen, Harrison, 1997, *Open Space Technology: a User's Guide*, Berrett-Koehler, San Francisco.

The ideogram of the old city is the enclosure; the ideogram of the old organization is the organization chart. The ideogram of the new city is the underground map, the rail network or the highway chart[15]; the ideogram of the new organization is the network. The citizen of the old organization lives in a box on the organization chart, only occasionally getting out of the box to talk to another resident in a bigger box called 'team'. The citizen of the new organization is a rider of the network, moving around and talking to other loose connections, some of them with stronger ties than others. Three 'B's reign in the old organization: boss, boundaries and bonuses. Three 'Is' reign in the new organization: influence, inter-dependence and innovation.

Having acknowledged that the hierarchical organization with its functional silos (which can be visible in companies of 5,000, 500 or 50 employees) had a bit of a problem in cross-communication, but not willing to kill the power silos altogether, the invention of the matrix as a cross-functional way of working was inevitable. It became a language key (we have a matrix system) and a clever hierarchical plot (I have two bosses: one local the other global). And the matrix became a very, very large petri dish for team meetings.

It was invented as a way to force people out of their dwellings to work together with other people (who were also forced out of their own dwellings). It sometimes

---

[15] Mitchell, William J, 1996, *City of Bits: Space, Place, and the Infobahn*, The MIT Press, US

# The old city - the old company

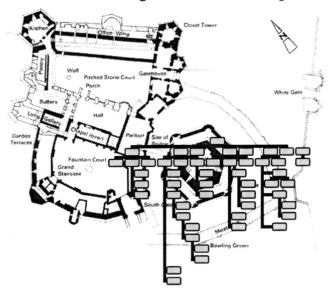

# The new city - the new company

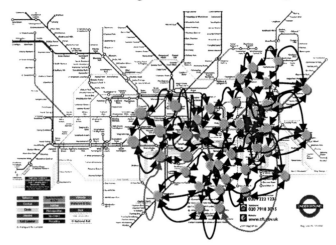

seemed that the conversation between them was just temporary and just long enough for somebody to look at his watch and exclaim: "*Oh, my God, so late already! I need to get back, bye*!" And back to their boxes they went...

# Riders and relationships

You don't need more team players. And I know you have just included this as part of the role spec for your new hires. I am going to guess that you already have lots of them. What you need big time are riders of networks. They create social capital when they breathe. Social capital is defined by the quantity and quality of your relationships (both personal and organizational), by your associability index (i.e., how many people you are associated with and how many want to be associated with you). Most of these associations are ad hoc and temporary.

Let me share my practical definition of a social capital index with you. You wake up in the middle of the night with a big issue in mind. How many people do you have on your contact list who can be called at 3.00 am to hear from you, "*Houston, we have a problem*!" and who are then willing to jump up and help? I know, it is an extreme definition, but you get the gist. (Incidentally, you tried this with Bob, Peter, Carol and Alice and it didn't work. They said, "*Just put it on the agenda*.")

Riders of the network navigate through connections inside and outside the organization. They lead from their own connectivity and ability to imagine their world as a vast space, mostly un-discovered. They are relationship builders, not team builders. They may not have a problem with teams and may even belong to some. But they tend to regard teams as the new silos.

Riders have meetings as well: 365/24/7 meetings. They are 'meeting up' all the time. It is their very 'raison d'être'. Riders want networkracy, not teamocracy. These new leaders will take the organization to territories where 'the answers' might be found and will do so via relationships, not through processes and systems. They are social-intelligent: a rare characteristic, often invisible in many layers of management or even in top leadership.

Navigation through social networks is often seen as something suspicious by the old citizens of the old city and the old organization. They are almost paranoid. They may call it politics, manoeuvring or anything else dubious. The concept of 'organizational politics' as negative and undesirable is well past its sell-by date. The new organization is politics; it is *polis*; it is relationships and mutual influence. It is not unethical manoeuvring; it is flow of conversations and influence that can only scare people who can't have a conversation or can't influence anybody.

# Recruitment briefing

We've done the team stuff. We have lots of them and they operate quite acceptably, thank you.

Before we implemented the matrix, we had seven divisions and seven silos. After implementing the matrix and creating the multidisciplinary team structure, we have seven non-silo divisions and 35 new team silos. We never solve the problems here; we just trade off between them.

We are looking for (social-intelligent) people able to establish a web of both internal and external relationships. Management has promised to keep a relatively low profile and let them roam relatively freely.

We acknowledge that, from time to time, we will have the temptation to declare some of them 'a team', but we promise we will refrain.

We are looking for people who can
demonstrate they can build
relationships.

We have a special interest in people
who founded a club at 11, created a
football team at 17 and put together a
bunch of friends to explore the Amazons
at 21. Or something like that.

## Profile:

- Social intelligence
- Connectedness
- Navigation skills (in any form)
- Hyper-linked
- Extra-structural management (we have reached our quota in intra-structure management)
- Relationship builders

## In the meantime in the office

- Institute a 'design tax': for each new team, introduce two facilitated forms of informal meetings (cookies provided)
- List people you have not seen in five or ten years and call them (find them)
- Send a how-are-you note to everybody in your stack of business cards, accumulated over the years at conferences and other places
- Practice social-networking using one of the multiple 'tools' available (if you don't know what I am talking about, ask your teenage daughter)

# [ EIGHT ]

# Chaordic acrobats

new leaders wanted: now hiring!

# Chaordic acrobats

## Ambiguity at the gates

The term 'chaordic' was invented by Dee Hock, father of the VISA organization, to describe the combination of (apparent) chaos and order.[16] He knew what he was talking about. He managed to create a multi-billion dollar enterprise without headquarters. Who is the CEO of VISA? There is no such thing. That federation of businesses works

---

[16] Hock, Dee W., 2000, *Birth of the Chaordic Age*, Berrett-Koehler, San Francisco; Hock, Dee W., 2005, *One from Many: VISA and the Rise of Chaordic Organization*, Berrett-Koehler, San Francisco

# chaos

from Latin. *chaos*. From Greek. *khaos* 'abyss, that which gapes wide open, is vast and empty'. 1606, 'utter confusion'.

# order

from Latin. *ordinem (nom. ordo)* 'row, rank, series, arrangement'. Originally 'a row of threads in a loom'; 'to arrange, arrangement'.

# ambiguous

From Latin. *ambiguus* 'having double meaning, shifting, changeable, doubtful'; 'to dispute about'. Lit. 'to wander'. From *ambi*- 'about' + *agere* 'drive, lead, act'.

very well with self-regulated and interconnected mechanisms, and that structure is far from traditional.

*Chaordism* is part of a broader reality which you and I would probably label 'ambiguity'. In those ambiguous realities - present in different degrees in many organizations - new leaders need to be acrobats. They will literally be acrobats of ambiguity. 'PhD in acrobatics' would be my desired and proposed qualification required.

Trouble is managers have not been trained for ambiguity, but for clarity. A job description is a job description; a team membership is a team membership and a department has clear boxes, lines and connections, as presented in the organization chart. No wonder we have a scarcity of skills on the 'navigating ambiguity' side. We don't have lots of people who are comfortable with the idea that things are not 100% clear and unequivocal, and that this is not necessarily a problem. There are several areas were ambiguity tends to pop up:

# 1. Boundaries

The modern organization is hardly a fortress. More and more, suppliers (and often customers) are intimately linked to the 'core' of the company. Relationships in the form of strategic collaborations, joint ventures, partnerships, co-marketing, etc. sometimes form a big web in which the recognition of strict borders becomes harder and harder. Some companies have equity interests in their competitors. Other companies have market value only through their alliances, not due to 'the core'. Some people belong to company A, but are paid by a legal entity bridge between companies A and B for the purposes of collaboration. Hardly citadel walls.

Very often, we also have confusion within the organization. People 'belonging' to a department may spend most of their time working on a project and their performance will mainly be assessed by the project leader, not by their 'real' boss. Some people have two bosses: one within their own function or the country manager and the other a global one, with both sometimes sitting an ocean apart. Some structures (teams, groups, committees) or projects may have some overlapping or shared responsibilities, or they may share a customer segment.

Wherever you look - and the above examples are mild - you are bound to find 'ambiguity'. Many managers spend a significant amount of work time trying to clarify these things because they can't really cope with ambiguity. But you need new leaders who are not only comfortable with this, but can navigate it and thrive on it.

The complexity of the organizational life is bound to produce a fair amount of ambiguity. If you don't like it, join the Army. You need the acrobats, not the stop-everything-and-clarify-for-me people. In fact, in trying to clarify, we have confused things more and invented multiple tricks to fool ourselves into feeling that it's all OK and crystal clear in the matrix.

## 2. Decisions and 'closure'

This is a tricky one where you desperately need those chaordic acrobats. In some organizations, decision making is weak, for example in the form of … no decision made when you are supposed to have one! This is bad. But the cure for this is often worse: let's make a decision and 'close the issue' as soon as we can. In my experience, I have seen more waste and issues arise from that. The need for 'closure' becomes such an urge that people 'close' everything on time, on target … and totally rubbish. It's a fine line, I know. The problem is that most of your work force doesn't see the fine lines, but only the thick, fat, bold ones. That's why you need the acrobats. These people have the ability to push for closure when needed one day and to suspend judgement another day. They're a rare species. They don't mind being called inconsistent. They are inconsistent by design. It's all in that PhD in Acrobatics.

## 3. Measurement

This is one of the most important issues in the organization today. People are asked to explain how they are going to measure success, how they are going to quantify changes, how they can numerically justify an investment to the ROI police. We have equated measurement with hard numbers and therefore, if we are not able to produce them, we risk being told that we are wasting our time. A leadership driven by numbers (and literally 'prisoner of these numbers') is very dangerous. Yet,

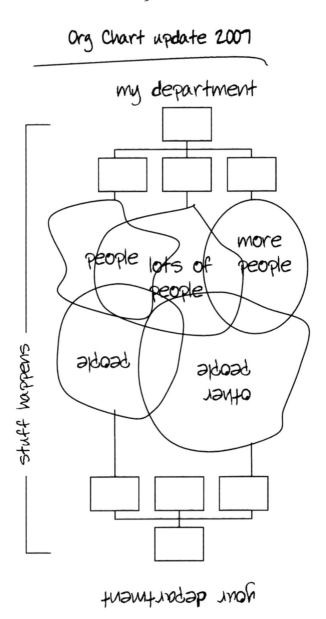

many organizations reward leaders for strict arithmetic outcomes. So, people end up fitting metrics everywhere, without even asking themselves the question: "*Are there different ways to track progress*?"

You may remember the donkeys of chapter two. Your acrobats see the donkeys. Your non-acrobats see chances to apply Six Sigma to the process of crossing international borders with a caravan of animals carrying bags, and they look forward to measuring the opportunity cost associated with a 10% reduction in the number of animals or the total number of bags per annum. "*It's donkeys, stupid*!" the acrobats shout. In many change processes, managers are so obsessed with measuring the changes that they don't notice the obvious.

In my work with organizations on change management (through *Viral Change*[17]), I emphasize the importance of stories as a vehicle of communication and understanding of what's going on. Some managers ask me, "*Can we quantify them*?" Of course you can. But what do you want? Total number? Percentage of good ones versus bad ones? Complete versus incomplete? Long awaited versus unexpected? Anecdotal versus widespread? I always tell them they can have anything they want; as long as they make sure they have time left to actually hear the stories. It's donkeys, you see? Again, chaordic acrobats are good at mixing hard and soft measures. They reject the Manichean

---

[17] Herrero, Leandro, 2006, *Viral Change: the alternative to slow, painful and unsuccessful management of change in organizations*, meetingminds, UK

world of either ROIs (at any cost, even on the back of an envelope if that satisfies the boss) or the fuzzy touchy-feely stuff. Einstein said that not everything that counts can be counted and not everything that can be counted counts. Amen to that.

## 4. 'Conversations'

Many organizations have lost the ability to hold open conversations that may or may not lead to a 'decision', an 'action' or 'closure'. There is no room for debate. Debate has been exiled from project team meetings. As soon as somebody engages in a conversation (debate) with somebody else, they are told to talk about it 'offline'. Conversations are also exiled from management and leadership teams. They are supposed to be a decision or sanctioning machinery. But conversations seem to follow the first law of thermodynamics: they never disappear, they just transform themselves.

Evicted from the natural places where they should be embraced, they find their way into the company cafeteria, into the corridors by the water cooler or in the 365/24/7 semi-invisible internal and external social networks, probably helped by some technology like blogs or chat rooms. Very recently, you may have seen blogs (open, external, public….) written by groups of employees talking about company issues, hiding under an anonymous personality, and often saying … well, not very nice things.

**140**

Open debate, playing with arguments, weighing the pros and cons, acknowledging that there may be no answer, parking the issue, revisiting it again, seeing it in a different way next week, etc. is seen as a waste of time and resources, a sign of lack of focus and, quite frankly, not a good way to get promoted.

But you need all that. It should be unthinkable to assume that people are like slot machines: insert the coin and get something ... or nothing. We hire people because of their talents and then, when they exhibit them, we ask them to talk offline, so as not to disturb the beautiful flow between item 7 and 8 of 'the agenda'.

You need chaordic acrobats able to navigate both the structured world of the agendas/decisions/actions and the informal world where ideas emerge and are cared for, possibilities are explored and imagination can roam free and remain playful (the latter considered chaos by structure-fundamentalists.) Actually, proficient chaordic acrobats go beyond feeling comfortable. They thrive on the co-existence of both models and can jump from one to another without any risk of a heart attack.

## Thresholds

This brings me to the topic of degrees and thresholds of ambiguity. This is the spectrum of progression: acknowledge (that ambiguity exists), embrace, utilize, foster and seek. Yes, that's right: seek! Seeking ambiguity may be a healthy measure when everything is absolutely clear! Somebody said that if managers have all the answers, then they probably didn't understand the questions. If everything runs smoothly, with pristine clarity, without debate and discussion in linear progression towards a beautiful solution ... something's not right. I had a client once who told his troops: "*If it feels OK, it's probably not good enough.*" It sounds like masochism, but it's far from that! It's just a healthy suspicion of permanent smoothness.

Our management education, whether formal or 'on-the-job', tells us that we should go to resolution fast, without wasting time, and feel proud of it. We are hooked on the aesthetics of completion. Managers are terrified of being seen as hosting open conversations, just in case they are asked the famous: "*What are you trying to achieve?*" To which they would have to reply, "*I don't know, but I'll see what happens.*" Your chaordic acrobats have gone past the terror and can navigate equally well through calm and stormy seas; through clear and foggy weather.

## The only ambiguity problem that needs fixing

Frustrated citizens of the organization express their frustration in numerous ways, but this 'Gang of Four' is by far more prominent than anything else. Fairness is one of the characters. People (or a team, or a division) perceive that they have not been treated fairly, that they have lost to somebody else. Consistency is the second character of the gang. If you do something one way and another similar thing in a different way, the claim is 'inconsistency'. When people say, for example, that a manager is 'inconsistent', this usually means they have difficulty predicting his actions. A manager may have solved a personnel issue one way and addressed another one completely different. Inconsistency is claimed. At that point character number one, fairness, jumps on the bandwagon and takes over. Now the action is unfair ... because it is inconsistent. The third character is clarity: what is it exactly that we need to do and, if possible, when, how, with whom and with which money? People sometimes complain that guidelines are not clear in that sense. Remember, it is a gang, so the other two inevitably join in. Now the lack of clarity reeks of unfairness and certainly shows gross inconsistency.

The fourth character is transparency. This is not the same as clarity. A manager can be very clear with his people, but other teams or the rest of the company may have little or no idea of what is going on. What they do is sometimes opaque, even if it's clear to them. At this point, the Gang of Four play together and now the terms are almost interchangeable. Something is wrong because it is inconsistent, unfair, unclear and far from transparent. And suddenly, you have a situation that will fuel conversations for the following few months.

If you think about it, there may be nothing wrong with each of the characters by themselves. Why should inconsistency be unfair? Inconsistency doesn't create unfairness; unfairness, however, may be consistent. Being unclear doesn't make it unfair, etc.

Chaordic acrobats have a special ability to dissect these four components, because they are not generally bothered by them (and this is a good diagnostic tool to find those people). They also tend to parachute into the company something that has the ability to handle a great deal of all the organizational problems and to look at all possible angles of ambiguity: accountability.

Chaordic acrobats do not compromise where accountability is concerned. You can say that this is the only item where tolerance to ambiguity should not exist. If you fix accountabilities, you can cope with many un-finished and un-clear business. Accountability is the ultimate fixer of the 'Gang of Four' problem. Chaordic acrobats know that.

The English language has two words that - when translated into other languages - translate into one and the same word: accountabilities and responsibilities. It has always surprised me how bad our use of those terms is in business English. In most of the conversations they end up as coterminous.

But the etymological roots are different. Accountability derives from 'counting', 'take (in)to account' and 'call to account'. Responsibility comes from 'responding', 'response', 'to respond'. But in other languages, there is only one term. Accountability in French is 'responsabilité', in Spanish 'responsabilidad', and in Italian 'responsabilita' … which translates back to … responsibility!

I suggest to people that there is a simple rule that will maximize the richness of the English distinction: accountability can't be shared (one person is 'called to account'); responsibility can be shared (many people may be responsible, responding to something.) Using this simple rule, you would get rid of much 'confusion' and many 'dilemmas'.

But still you need your chaordic acrobats to lead the overall ambiguity. If everything is crystal clear, chances are you are not ahead of the game.

# Recruitment briefing

We are seeking new leaders with high
tolerance for ambiguity, with
specialization in areas such as
strategy, HR, team development,
collaborations, joint ventures and
partnerships and general management.
In other words, pretty much everything.
We have done the black and white stuff
and have huge binders filled with job
descriptions and team charters that are
occupying too much shelf space.

We are seeking acrobats of ambiguity
who can bring some order to our chaotic
aspects and a bit of chaos to our
orderly and predictable processes. Our
traditional borders between core and
non-core, internal and external
networks, us and our partnerships, us
and our suppliers are foggy to say the
least. We have plenty of people who
could solve the ambiguity problem by
killing all ambiguity. But we need
people who can thrive on this.

## Profile:

- Accepts the fog, lands anyway
- Ambiguity management does not create severe health problems for them
- Sees possibilities in both the structured and unstructured side of things
- Crosses boundaries without creating internal diplomatic incidents
- Thinks that having two bosses is not enough. Wants at least three, so he has more possibilities of influencing senior people
- Previous experience as a bishop or squadron commander automatically disqualifies for this job

# In the meantime in the office

- Establish a comfortability index for issues, projects and activities. The higher the comfort, the more suspicious you should be (but first you must put all the masochists into therapy)
- Make a point of distinguishing between accountability (not shared) and responsibility (can be shared)
- Protect debate space
- Allow free floating conversations
- Have both meetings with and without closure on issues and refrain from calling the latter a waste
- Ask your ROI police how they would calculate the ROI for love, looking at a piece of art, friendship, trust or employee pride. If the answer is unsatisfactory, fire them

# [ NINE ]

# Disruptors

new leaders wanted: now hiring!

# Disruptors

## Managing by default

Many organizations work in default mode. Nothing intrinsically wrong with that and many of them are successful. They function in an orderly way. There is a sense of manufactured coherence in the air. Their management is prêt-a-porter management, straight from the shelves of 'Universal Standard Practices' or 'United Colours of Management'. "*But it works!*" people claim.

'Managing' means a series of activities that managers perform, following explicit or implicit rules. One is not usually left to 'manage as one wishes' or in one's true personal style. There is a hidden message: do not reinvent

# disruption

from Latin.
*disruptionem*, from stem
of *disrumpere* 'break
apart, split'. From *dis-*
'apart' + *rumpere* 'to
break'.

the wheel, just do what good managers do. As soon as the title of 'manager' is adjudicated to somebody, he enters a ritual performance where the script is already largely written for him. The manager de facto becomes part of the 'tribe of managers' and he is trained in what he is expected to do as manager.

Managing in many cases has also mostly become managing the inevitable. Internal processes and systems are intricate and require a great deal of energy and attention. Sometimes, as much as 90% of all that company energy and attention is focused internally, whilst only 10% is looking at the customer or the external world. (A) We have meetings, make decisions and write minutes; (B) things happen (or perhaps better à la Don Rumsfeld: stuff happens) and so, (C) we are managing. That trilogy of the inevitable is established as coterminous with 'organizational life'. The Managing-by-Default School of Management has one objective in mind: the domestication of organizational life. This may or may not be articulated in this way (it probably won't), but that goal is mostly part of that unconscious life of the organization which writes the rules in secret before they are even uncovered and written by managers.

## Best Practices = 'Me-Too' Practices

An organization worth the title 'good organization', may also have 'Best Practices': a combination of ideas, standards, processes and systems that have worked and still work well and are comparable with others via some sort of benchmarking, perhaps external to the company. The whole idea behind them is repetition. In the modern organization, 'Best Practices' is a term that is more and more used in a generic way, almost equivalent to 'the way we do things here' or 'the high standards of our processes'. Best Practices easily become 'Me-Too' Practices. In fact, the average company is a 'me-too' company. Kjell Nordström and Jonas Ridderstråle have expressed it well: "*The 'surplus society' has a surplus of similar companies, employing similar people, with similar educational backgrounds, working in similar jobs, coming up with similar ideas, producing similar things, with similar prices and producing similar quality*"[18] Depressing, I know.

The whole act of managing has to do with incorporating the best possible way of doing things. The Best Practices fashion has made people move in that laudable direction. It has also prompted some to open the windows of the organization and see what's going on elsewhere, what other best practice can be applied. It is hard to see what could be wrong with this approach. But, however needed, it is not sufficient, assuming you want to get out of the 'me-too' box. And this is a colossal assumption I am making here.

Success breeds complacency, we tend to say. It brings a dangerous legitimization of the way we do things. (A) We have Best Practices, (B) we do well, so the

---

[18] Ridderstråle, Jonas, Nordström, Kjell A., 2002, *Funky Business: Talent Makes Capital Dance*, Financial Times Management, UK

conclusion is that (C) we do well because we have Best Practices. The Managing-by-Default School of Management does not teach prevention of these post-hoc fallacies. In fact, the Managing-by-Default School of Management encourages them. Management has become the art of linking pieces to give them causality status. Reduction in personnel, reorganization and an increase in market share, for example, mean an increase in market share thanks to the cleaned up and lean newly organized company. Stuck on something? Introduce a new CEO and the earnings per share (EPS) go up. So, the new CEO is excellent at delivering rising EPS. Massive training and communication programme on customer focus followed by better market performance? The customer has responded and our training and communication programme is best practice. And so on. We love to be fooled by randomness[19].

## Disruption (= discontinuity) required

Unless you want your organization to continue the journey towards the Oscar for Best 'Me Too' Company (totally compatible with a nomination for 'Most Admired Corporation'), you need to inject something into the management structure and processes. You need to inject instability. Yes, this is not a typo. And you need to have new leaders of the disruptor type. The first thing that comes to our mind when we hear 'disruption' is chaos. And yet

---

[19] Taleb, Nassim Nicholas, 2001, *Fooled by Randomness: The Hidden Role of Chance in the Markets and in Life*, Texere LLC, NY

dictionaries define disruption as 'an act of delaying or interrupting the continuity'.

Whilst the majority of the organization follows the insanity rule ('continue doing the same things in the same old way and expecting different results'), you need leaders who can inject enough disruption to take you away from the linearity of the predictable. And by doing so, give your organization a chance to win via differentiation and innovation. These disruptors share some of the following characteristics:

## 1. Challenging the status quo

They are uncomfortable with the continuity in the pervasive progression of more of the same. They challenge the default position by saying, "*This is how we have always done it. Could there be a better way? We have solved this crisis, we are all happy. Are we becoming proficient in solving crises instead of in avoiding them?*"

## 2. No contention, no progress

Connected to the above, disruptors challenge conventional thinking, perhaps just because it is conventional. They are not saying conventional is wrong. They are saying it is not enough and it will not take you beyond the 'me-too' status. Disruptors sometimes come up with counterintuitive questions and views. They have a special ability to ask 'what if'. Yes, they may be irritating at times, but you need to host these irritations and canalize them properly.

## 3. Taking risks

Disruptors have a different concept of risk. They are by far less risk averse than anybody else. After all, there is no disruption without risk. They see risk as progress and avoiding risk as a death certificate. It is quite common to find people who seem to have achieved high or semi-high office by taking the least possible risks. They have no mistakes to declare. They are anti-disruptors. Because of their status, they may constitute role models, sometimes of an unconscious nature. You need disruptors now. They may look pretty different from your leadership DNA, so you'll need to find them, seduce them, hire and 'protect' them. You must ask for their contribution to increase un-conformability levels. But you have to be very aware that if you ask … you just might get it.

## 4. Engaging contradiction

You may have created, or work in, a pretty predictable and disciplined organization with lots of logic and rationality. This kind of organization, following a rather mechano-hydraulic model, doesn't like contradictions. For example, it says that you can't have Strategy A *and* B if B is contradictory to A. That may be the case. But because no possibility of contradiction is ever allowed, everything that *is* accepted gets the blessing of being non-contradictory.

**158**

Contradiction and its sister, irrationality, are at the core of the imagination. Disruptors have the ability to assume contradictions and test them in contexts that you may not (want to) see from the traditional view. They don't close the conversation at that early point of 'closure' where you have decided to go with B (and have therefore automatically ruled out A). They will make the point of exploring A as well, in a way that will perhaps irritate sound and solid people. Disruptors seem to have an aversion to what has been called 'the tyranny of the or'[20]: the common or conventional thinking that says you must choose between A and B as you can't have both.

Be aware that there are always people in the organization who want 'everything'. These are not the disruptors. On the contrary, these are people who want to play all the cards and play it safe. They don't make a lot of judgements, whilst disruptors first push the contradictory and contrarian thinking through and then happily progress in one direction. If it were up to them, probably the riskier one.

## 5. Seeking dissidents and deviants

Because of all the above, disruptors tend to look for dissidents and people who deviate from the norm. Some of those may achieve good results in ways that are unconventional.

---

[20] Collins, James C., Porras, Jerry I, 2004, *Built to Last: Successful Habits of Visionary Companies*, Harper Collins, NY

There are two groups of dissidents and deviants. The first is composed of people who get away with murder in order to achieve organizational benefit, but they will do this mainly for personal glorification. The second group may also look like they're getting away with murder, but the personal benefit, ego building and selfish approach is not immediately obvious. Deviants of the second group simply bypass bureaucracy, find shortcuts through layers of authority, get on with things, bend some rules and, in general, do things 'differently'. But they always do so with organizational and business goals in mind. The first group is bad news, and when management turns a blind eye to them ... it's even worse news.

The first group is well-represented in sales organizations where a subgroup of individuals become 'untouchable' because of their 'performance' (=making money), even if they exhibit behaviours that are in total contradiction with the Directives on Values and Attitudes of the last Company Retreat. Disruptors will have no time for this first group, but they will connect very well with the second. They see deviance as a source of learning[21], not as something to dismiss. A significant contribution to the rise in value of social deviance was made by fieldworkers for Save the Children. They spotted that in areas of poverty and malnutrition, there was always a group of children that didn't suffer from malnutrition, even though they shared the same environment and resources. The fieldworkers looked at the mothers' feeding habits and found that they did some

---

[21] Herrero, Leandro, 2004, Article: *Benchmarking Deviance* (Can be found and read at http://www.thechalfontproject.com/ideaslab.htm)

things differently. For example, they gathered unusual 'foods' from rivers and fields; things that were generally discarded by the majority as 'not edible'. This 'deviant behaviour' was the source of success for those children and their families.

# The beginners' mind

Any organization will have a small percentage of dissident, deviants, unorthodox and other 'abnormal' people who are usually just a bit of a pain. Disruptors overlap with that community, but are no addition to it. Disruptors are leaders and are not just (if at all) wild, unmanageable, unpredictable, uncomfortable and painful people for the sake of being different. It is a fine line, but the more you seduce and hire disruptors, or the more time you spend time in their company, the better you'll become at drawing those lines.

Disruptors may share some characteristics with the wild and restless, but they are organizationally and business focussed. Disruptors are also the representation of the anti-expert. A Zen Master said: "*In the beginners' mind, there are many possibilities; in the experts' mind, there are few*". You may have all the experts, but now you need some beginners.

# Innovation, incrementalism and disruptors

Disruption is a condition for innovation and "*incrementalism is innovation's worst enemy*", as Nicholas Negroponte – founder of MIT's media lab – said. I know that many people have adopted the term 'incremental innovation', but this kind of overlaps with 'continuous improvement'. Truly real innovation - with a capital I - is not incremental. It is not about inventing a motor to make a bicycle run when the question is about driving a Ferrari. I know it sounds a bit harsh, but I don't think you can have real innovation as long as you have your processes, systems, structures and people all geared towards improving things bit by bit.

Nature and physics have something in common: a struggle between continuity and discontinuity. And business has only recently paid attention to this, pre-occupied as it was with changing the oil of the machines of continuous improvement. Today, this is a question of balance and energy. Nobody would negate the importance of improvement, but if this is the *only* thing you are aiming at, you may be missing one or two things. Whilst you probably have plenty of the old skills that will ensure continuous improvement, you need the disruptors to challenge things and to aim at 'jumps' in the evolution curve of the company.

**162** |

# Recruitment briefing

We are a largely stable organization that has grown over the years by the implementation of successful strategies and Best Practices.

We are in part a 'company of experts', where Centres of Excellence have been developed to host those 'experts', both on the commercial and technical sides. We have created a large, collective, mechanical mind where the power of the 'expert logic' prevails.

We are looking for a bit of disruption and the ability to ask non-expert, difficult, unconventional and possibly annoying questions. All the easy ones were already answered a while ago.

We want people who can see all the possibilities instead of just one world; who can actually live in several worlds at the same time and who can bring the unconventional thinking to the party.

new leaders wanted: now hiring!

All people with a good track record of effective disruption will be considered, even if totally ignorant of our business.

Please note: resumes without a descriptive list of mistakes will be shredded instantly.

## Profile:

- Challenges the status quo
- Takes risks (please demonstrate)
- Un-reasonable people
- Asks difficult questions
- Learns from deviance
- Seeks discontinuity
- Anti-default position thinker
- Sees 'progress' as discontinuity, healthy conflict and perhaps controversy
- All the above may be uncomfortable for others, but they don't capitalize on that pain or seek disruption for the sake of it
- Possibly alien to our industry
- Needs to show at least one instance where their disruption made a difference, which can be anywhere and anytime between kindergarten and now

# In the meantime in the office

- Test any 'or' strategy against the possibility of an 'and' strategy, even if that has been discarded from the start
- Review all your 'non-starter' strategies or initiatives and ask why they were labelled as such
- Look for deviants and invite them to strategic meetings
- Practice 'what if'
- Have routine post-mortem meetings asking if there were possible different ways of doing things
- Look at both successes and bottlenecks and try to see what could have happened if disruptive thinking had been applied
- Define the degree of 'me-too' in your organization (and don't be fooled by the presence of those 'innovative products')
- Look at all your 'default' positions (which in computer sciences means 'standard', but stands for 'failure to act' etymologically speaking)

# [ TEN ]

# Butterfly Managers

new leaders wanted: now hiring!

# Butterfly Managers

## The tsunami and the butterfly

In my book, *Viral Change* (meetingminds, 2006), I make the distinction between two models of change management: the tsunami and the butterfly. Most change processes - whether formal 'change management programmes' or routine 'management of change' - are tsunamis. They start at the top with the key messages of goals and objectives, and cascade down the organization, progressively increasing the size of both the waves and the

# management

1598, 'act of managing'
from *manage*. 'Governing
body' (originally of a
theater). Also, 'one who
conducts a house of
business or public
institution'.

# manage

1561, from Italian.
*maneggiare* 'to handle'.
Also 'to control a horse',
from Latin *manus* 'hand'.

# influence

From Latin. *influentia* 'a
flowing in'; *influere* 'to
flow into'. From *in-* 'in' +
*fluere* to flow'.

stack of PowerPoints. Presidents brief Vice Presidents, VPs have retreats with Directors, Directors brief Managers, Managers brief the troops. The theory says it's a fairly standard process. All that is needed is a clear set of objectives, a clear rationale, an explanation of the reasons for the change, good communication packages that reach every single corner of the organization, appropriate training for 'the new ways' (particularly if there are new processes and systems) and then ... well, people will just follow accordingly and change.

This sequential model hasn't changed for years, but the fact is, most change management programmes fail. The reason? This model assumes many things:

One:   you need to make sure you reach everybody in the organization with the universal communication programme.

Two:   the whole process is rational: explain why the changes are needed and people will just follow and change.

Three: big problems need big solutions. So, this means big changes.

Four:  it's going to be a long and difficult process because (a) people are resistant to change and (b) it takes time for the changes to be established and become embedded.

## Shaky pillars

All the above assumptions are flawed. Reaching everybody with a massive communication tsunami assumes that information delivered equals information understood and/or internalized, and/or a trigger for change. Nothing could be further from reality. Only a fraction of the organization understands the information and only a fraction of that fraction will actually change as a direct consequence of the information received. Rationality is also a very dangerous assumption. People may be able to understand things rationally, but may not be able to internalize them emotionally, let alone change their behaviours accordingly.

Big problems may not need big solutions. Organizational life is full of people with 75 objectives, strategic plans with 20 implementation goals and 20x4 critical success factors, change programmes with 10 parallel initiatives, divided into 3 senior-sponsored task forces and multiple action plans. We let ourselves be overwhelmed by the magnificence of the tsunami. We also kid ourselves if we think that success is the sum of 75 objectives achieved, 20 implementation milestones reached and 80 critical success factors managed.

Actually, the bigger the problems, the greater the chances that a small set of underlying issues are at the core of them. These could be tackled by the introduction of an equally small set of new behaviours or key drivers which, if reinforced properly, will have the power to deal with everything and create massive change faster and in a more sustainable way. In my work with organizations, I call these 'non-negotiable behaviours'. This behavioural model is also valid and very successful for so-called 'cultural change' since behaviours shape culture, not the other way around.

It doesn't have to be painful either. We make it painful and miserable because this is what we expect and what we have been taught to expect. In particular, we assume that people have some sort of genetic predisposition to resist change. And many people cling to the mantra 'people are resistant to change', especially people with academic and consulting backgrounds, who tend to do so with extraordinary energy. In reality, and from a biological viewpoint, we are not resistant to change, because we *are* change! No baby resists becoming a child and no child resists becoming an adolescent: it just happens. Life and change are synonymous.

What we see is people behaving as if they resist. But instead of asking ourselves why, we stop there and assume that people just *are* resistant. It becomes a fantastic alibi to justify the failure of lousy change management programmes! The reality is that people react in a resistant way when they can't control the whole or parts of the change. Multiple animal experiments have shown that there is a significant difference in outcome between being able to avoid or control some pain and just being a passive recipient of unpleasant actions. Animals in the second scenario develop all sorts of problems including ulcers. In the first scenario, they don't ... because they have some control over the circumstances.

## Talk less, do more

In tsunami mode you get tsunami managers. You can spot them by the size of their PowerPoint presentations, their communication plans (including Town Hall meetings, a GE export, etc.) and their affinity for off-site gatherings. And you can spot them easily, because they are visible, very visible. In fact, they explain the changes themselves, lead the workshops and speak at their all-company conferences.

But there is an alternative to the tsunami: it is Butterfly Management. In Butterfly Management mode, managers deal with a small set of initiatives or behaviours and use the power of influence between individuals to spread the necessary changes (which can be anything from new ideas, new processes, new ways of doing to new behaviours that can shape a desired new culture).

Whilst the tsunami approach assumes that everybody in the organization is equal in their capacity to listen, understand, integrate and change, Butterfly Management accepts that only a small number of individuals in the organization have the power to influence others and/or start a chain of influence. Butterfly Managers work with those networks of influence, either pre-existing and natural ones or those created by 'change activists' or 'change leaders'.

# The art of backstaging

Butterfly Managers perform the art of back-staging. Like the flutter of a butterfly's wings has the power to create a storm miles away, the backstage - and sometimes even invisible - actions of Butterfly Managers have the power to trigger a chain of imitation and social copying with widespread consequences. In Butterfly Management mode, 'change management' is closer to the creation of internal infections. This is the goal, not the conventional linear appeal to rationality and the sequential implementation of 'the six steps' (for change) or any other mechanistic model. This is what Butterfly Managers do:

## 1. Influence: it's personal

They influence their immediate network by first endorsing the necessary changes and role modelling them. Next, they engage others when the new behaviours are present and/or new processes are running. This is very often done through pure peer-to-peer influence. Some of those Butterfly Managers are 'natural', i.e. were born that way. They understand the power of small interventions crafted in the background and then spread via networks of influence. In my *Viral Change* model, I tend to identify people in the organization who have this natural power of influence, so I effectively try to find those individuals. There are many ways to do it. In many cases, the organization already seems to know these people very well.

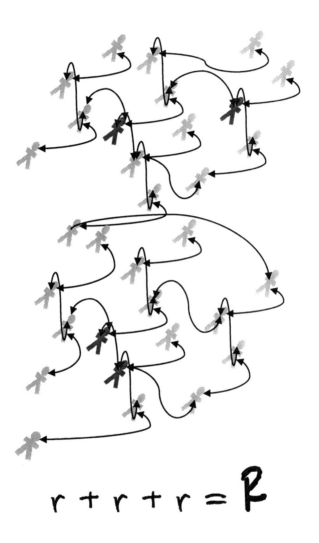

r + r + r = R

## 2. Mobilize commitment

They mobilize internal commitment, which is often hidden or not tapped into. They are infectors themselves and tend to energize other people. Chances are they infect their immediate network first, and that network then repeats it with their own network circle. At some point, 'the change' will have enough critical mass to reach a tipping point and become 'the norm'. Butterfly Managers do not pretend that everybody is ready and equal, so the idea of a universal communication programme with cascaded workshops across the board is completely alien to them. They treat the triggering of commitment and energy as an infection that starts somewhere (in most cases with them) and spreads out the way infections do: first infecting those who are ready to receive it! As I said before, massive communication and training programmes often fail because there is no differentiation between recipients. Able, unable, ready, immune, high-level-of-antibodies ... all are treated the same in the tsunami.

## 3. Distributed leadership

They practice a form of leadership that is distributed across the organization, although they may not call it like this. And distributed doesn't simply mean geographically dispersed. Sure, it includes that, but it also means synergic and synchronous action, i.e. the power of simultaneous leadership actions as pockets of influence. The classical non-distributed leadership (at the top, in the hierarchical management levels of the organization chart) has its liabilities, because it assumes a mechanistic organization of bits and pieces. The modern network-structured organization (which, by the way, still keeps an organization chart alive so the company still looks 'explainable') can't rely on those hierarchical boxes: there is leadership all over the place, acting simultaneously. And the official-leadership-at-the-top role is to keep this alive and well and to make sure that the distributed leadership engine is fully supported.

## 4. r+r+r=R

This is the Butterfly Management equation: small radical changes add up to create Big Radical Change. Butterfly Managers understand this very well. They are good at 'the small r stuff' but, don't fool yourself, they always have the big R in mind. Remember the widespread assumption that big issues require big interventions, big programmes, big actions, big budgets … i.e. big changes? This is a result of our linear thinking which is programmed into our brains from as early as kindergarten and which gets reinforced from then on.

However, our social world (and that includes organizations) is full of non-linear (dynamics) mechanisms where small actions provoke catastrophes and single events trigger wars. Luckily, Butterfly Managers seem to have antibodies against linearity.

# Multi-issues and multi-programmes

Butterfly Managers are part explorers and part epidemiologists. As explorers, they try to find the key levers of many things, the tree in the forest of issues or activities. As accidental epidemiologists, they will use the spread of social infection to create the changes which are not associated with the Big List of Issues, but with the small set of underlying 'causes'. As an example, imagine a company where sales people under-use the electronic system to track customer activity, their Customer Relationship Management (CRM) system. They literally feed very little back into that system, which is supposed to be used by all their fellow salesmen. It is a self-reinforcing mechanism, leading to less and less use because people can find less and less data and utility. Imagine now that same organization sensing that they need teamwork because teams are not working. They may say, for example, that it's a 'cultural problem'. Perhaps the same organization is also not very good at having functions talking to each other. Marketing, Sales, Operations and R&D are silos handing things over the fence from time to time. It is their 'silo problem'.

A conventional 'change management' programme would identify these three issues, would spend some time understanding the causes and would plan 'change management initiatives', possibly in these terms:

a. Enhancement of the CRM system and process improvement programme to increase participation. Key activities: gather everybody and make sure

## Tsunami Management of Change

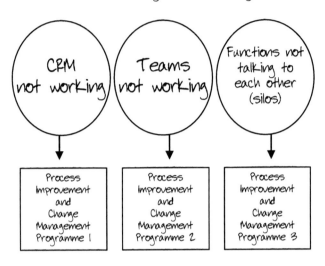

## Butterfly Management of Change

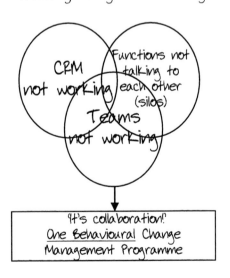

that they understand the importance of using the system and its benefits. Train them again. Duration: six months. Sponsor: Head of Sales Force Effectiveness.

b. A Corporate Team Effectiveness Programme. Key activities: Training programme on teamwork, including the importance of teams, the progression towards high performance teams, the dysfunctional teams and the leadership of teams. Programme starts at national level and descends to regional and local, eventually involving all declared teams. Duration: one year. Sponsor: Head of HR.

c. Cross-Functional Team Building Programme. Key activities: mixed Marketing, Sales, Operations and R&D workshops to understand each other and create a sense of team. Each group presents to others what they do, what their challenges are, etc. Activity to be repeated 3 months later with some assignments in between. Sponsor: Head of Marketing.

To which Butterfly Managers respond: "*It's collaboration, stupid!*" The three 'problems' have the same underlying behavioural cause: lack of collaboration. If collaboration is not part of the company's behavioural fabric/DNA, the CRM System Improvement Programme, the Corporate Team Effectiveness Programme and the Cross-Functional Team Building Programme are bound to fail. Plus, these programmes are introduced alongside the other dozen or so corporate/company initiatives running in parallel, which logarithmically increases the scepticism levels[22]. Butterfly Managers would focus on installing 'collaboration' as a behaviour first and then deal with the specific manifestations of the lack of it.[23]

Imagine how your organization would work with the existence of a scattered network of Butterfly Managers as described above…. Butterfly Managers will use influence and promote imitation. They are far less visible, occupy a far smaller number of high level power positions, talk less and do more. Their change capacity is immense. Whilst influence mechanisms as a concept are very much present in many marketing, advertising and consumer behaviours analyses, as far as its application *inside* the organization is concerned, it is vague, underused, underdeveloped and often nothing more than a rather theoretical idea embedded in the concept of leadership.

You need these butterfly people. Their potential to shape change in a fast and sustainable way is one of the best kept secrets of organizational life. I hope you find them fast.

---

[22] Herrero, Leandro, 2006, Article: *New Initiative? Sure, whatever* (Can be found and read at www.thechalfontproject.com/ideaslab.htm)
[23] These principles and its practical implications are dealt with more elaborately in *Viral Change* (meetingminds, 2006)

## Recruitment briefing

Our organization has had its fair bit of change management programmes over the last five years, all of them with different degrees of success. We have tried all possible communication systems, created seamlessly cascading workshops and established an Office of Change Management with its own Director and Managers.

Despite all these efforts, we have a problem: our changes don't stick.

We are now looking for leaders who can influence more quietly and create 'an internal epidemic of success' without having to re-start the same conventional change management show again.

Our people have become rather cynical about 'yet another change management programme'. We feel that we can achieve more by doing more and talking less.

People who need extreme visibility when leading an initiative don't need to apply (it's nothing personal, just a question of space: we have lots of those already).

People with previous roles as Heads of Corporate Project Management or Six Sigma warriors will also be at a disadvantage.

## Profile:

- Backstaging, stage management, working in the back room
- Leading quietly
- Mobilizes commitment and energy (as opposed to sucks energy from others)
- Small 'r' proficiency
- Action oriented (as opposed to talking oriented)
- Role modelling
- Takes influence seriously, even 'personally' (those who think this is 'politics' don't need to apply)
- Has shown examples of their 'stage management' abilities and can articulate achievements obtained with little personal visibility

## In the meantime in the office

- Find your influencers
- Don't start the planned Next Big Change Management Programme. First stop and think (or it becomes 'There we go again!')
- Cut all-encompassing corporate 'initiatives' by half (and I'm being conservative here)
- Discover/uncover your own behavioural fabric. Try to see if it is the source of multiple issues and problems

# [ ELEVEN ]

# Conquistadores

new leaders wanted! now hiring!

# Conquistadores

## Terra incognita

Welcome to this mixed bag representing people who are willing to take the organization beyond the borders of the known! I know, it sounds pretty scary. Would you really want to have these people around? I can just hear some of you, "*No thanks, life is challenging enough as it is!*" However…, the future depends on people who are able to think the unthinkable and imagine that future. They could be anywhere in your organization: at top, medium or even very low levels. You need them. And if you feel that you are short of this species, you'll have to hop on your bike and go find them.

# conquer

From Latin. *conquirere*
'to search for, procure'.
Also, 'to seek, acquire'.
Related to query, from
Latin *quære* 'ask', 'to
seek, gain'. Related to
inquiry.

# conquistador

Spanish (1830) 'conqueror'
Also related to query.

Whilst the rest of the organization is happy to populate, design, redesign and play in the familiar territory of 'terra cognita', conquistadores are willing to travel to the 'incognita', the unexplored, the wild unknown. Don't get too spooked by semi-New-Age-terminology. I am talking new markets, new geographies, new business models, new possibilities ... all pretty terrestrial stuff.

Conventional business school education would say, "*Oh, do you perhaps mean horizontal and vertical integration?*" No, I mean 'terra incognita', explored with passion by a few bearded guys with helmets and some ships. I can't imagine myself waking up in the morning and thinking to myself: "*Today, I am going to explore vertical integration and maximization of the value chain.*" Organizational conquistadores have a mission: discovery, not an MBA exam.

But these kinds of people are hard to pin down. We recognize them when we see them. Sometimes it happens a posteriori, after the new territory has been discovered. To create a psychological profile of these new leaders, I will use 10 keywords, like 10 cooking ingredients, and any combination of these will lead you to different dishes, all with a distinct conquistador flavour:

## 1. Discovery

Conquistadores believe that there are still territories worth discovering. They may or may not be close to home. The easy ones are the so-called 'expansions' (vertical and horizontal integrations, geographical, etc.), but there may be others which are not that obvious. They have a sense of possibilities and feel that the current reality may just be a bit of a trap for their organization.

## 2. Curiosity and inquiry

This is a wonderful gift that this kind of individual possesses. They ask lots of questions! It is the ability to go beyond the obvious and to try and understand the variety of mechanisms that may be behind what otherwise may look and sound like normal day-to-day practices. I am talking about success taken for granted, a failure that leads to quickly reacting and giving up some options, uncomfortable customer feedback that is dismissed as statistics, etc. Conquistadores are restless users of the 'why?' They seem to have an inquisitorial mind and carry on inquiring when everybody else has already stopped, fully satisfied.

## 3. Explorers

The explorer-within takes these kinds of leaders to several different pathways, never to just one. They have the instinctive belief that multiple ways lead to multiple places. The rest of the organization settles for one way to get to the destination, which is pretty much fixed in the 500-page strategic plan. In the eyes of the latter group, explorers seem to be wasting their time, to say the least, venturing into possibilities and 'what ifs' that, surely, 'the company' (usually referred to as 'they') will never accept. But still those conquistadores keep looking at options!

**192**

## 4. Mapmaking

This is a fine art. Conquistadores rely on maps, but if these don't exist (which is a pretty good signal of a territory - market, business model, etc. - worth conquering), they will make one, as cartography is another special gift of these people. A map usually doesn't give you one single way. That suits the conquistador, who likes to keep several options open. Plus, a map also tells you something about the distance between where you are and the terra incognita.

Conquistadores build plans to travel to those new territories, but - due to the very nature of the unknown - they will never stick to a dogmatic view of the journey. I have explored this facet of leadership in my book, *The Leader with Seven Faces* (meetingminds, 2006), as one of the key aspects of leadership, one that emphasizes the journey as opposed to having fixed ideas on the destination ('the vision thing').

## 5. Travellers

This characteristic may seem like a given, but in organizational terms it means exactly that: to travel, do it, move ... as opposed to writing numerous strategic plans based on tons of market research data from your office on the $10^{th}$ floor, executive wing. Travelling is not virtual travelling via PowerPoint reality: it is real field trips. New leaders with this 'traveller' characteristic are more

new leaders wanted! now hiring!

anthropologists than Board Directors. They need to see, feel and smell. That may entail time spent in fringe territories (completely different business) to put themselves in real terra incognita (for them). Imagine somebody senior from a pharmaceutical company, for example, spending a month working at Google and you'll get the gist of the kind of travel I am talking about. I didn't mean inviting some Google people to come and present at the offsite gathering as an oddity and curiosity disguised as learning, but in practical terms being nothing but pure entertainment.

## 6. Imagination

Here we hit another one of those features that prompts prudent people to be 'careful' just in case these people bring 'too much'. It's only in the business world that I have found this idea that one can have too much imagination. Imagination can't be forced or booked into Outlook as a Wednesday afternoon session. Most people probably do not use it enough. Some because they have been told that they don't have it, as if imagination is something that one does or does not possess. Others because the pathways in front of them are so well laid out that 'imagination is not required'. New leaders with great talent for imagination allow themselves to wander. They need to be protected, in the same way you need to protect space and time (see chapter three).

## 7. Restless minds

There are two kinds of restless minds: the healthy restless type and the pathological one. Another fine line, though. New leaders of the restless mind type have that kind of healthy restlessness that is a bit contagious. They are not satisfied easily, but they are not the kind that is never satisfied. Their restlessness is the energy that allows them to explore, to travel, to inquire, to discover, to imagine.

You have perhaps met people who seem to be in a rather permanent state of impatience about business decisions, actions, implementations, etc. Sometimes, they may have made you uncomfortable. Other times, you may have welcomed their presence. You need this ingredient somewhere in the organization as a vaccination against complacency and lack-of-sense-of-urgency: a pathology easily developed in many companies. Their minds may sometimes seem like 'a tree full of monkeys' (i.e. jumping all over the place), but you are better off with this type than with the alternative: the already dead with death certificate pending.

## 8. Adventure

Again this is another overlapping feature. Look at what dictionaries show us: escapade, risky venture, dangerous undertaking (a wild and exciting undertaking, not necessarily lawful), gamble, risk, hazard, take a chance/risk (in the hope of a favourable outcome), etc. I would emphasize the 'taking risks' component, which has come up before. As an example, going for vertical integration, a logical acquisition or a geographical expansion next door may be a terribly good thing to do, but, generally, I would not call it an adventure. The adventure type of new leaders will take risks and go beyond the predictability of normal organizational life.

## 9. Quest

A quest is pursuing something. It is a sense of destiny. And before you think of this as a grandiose idea with no place in organizational life, I invite you to think of destiny with a small d. I am not talking about liberating a country dressed like Ghandi or about saving the planet. I am talking about a sense that the organization has reached a point where it can excel at something, achieve something significant, leave a specific, reasonable legacy. It may be a quest for quality, for uniqueness in customer interaction or for innovation.

The difference between a quest and strategic objectives is that 'quest' incorporates a search and the drive to find. It has the conquistador flavour that the often bland, naked, clinical and unemotional strategic objectives don't offer. You need new leaders in a quest mood as part of your pool of conquistadores. You probably already have the other ones.

## 10. 'In transit'

New leaders 'in transit' mode are 180 degrees removed from the ones who 'have reached a destination'. Always being 'in transit' is a healthy position in organizational life. It means constantly moving, walking, travelling and on a quest for a better performance, whichever way you define that. 'In transit' is also a state of mind, an attitude towards continuously moving forward. New leaders 'in transit' create that sense of movement, which is partly contagious and partly a reminder that the journey matters and that you'll never reach the destination completely. 'In transit' is another good vaccination against complacency.

## All the above

Conquistadores are made of a mixture of all these traits and only differ from each other by the percentage of the ingredients used. You need most of them for a good dish, but 'the spirit of conquest' is the common denominator.

You need new leaders with the passion to explore and conquer new territories. By definition, these conquistadores are masters of strategies, not strategy. And these are also dynamic and adaptable. However, conquistadores have been known to make these strategies less adaptable in favour of total commitment to the cause. Example: Cortés leadership. He arrives in Mexico and burns his ships so there is no doubt about his intentions. Sometimes, conquistadores need to make a point!

As I have mentioned before, there is nothing theoretical about these traits. New conquistador-style leaders have their feet firmly on the ground. They are not thinking of conquering. They conquer. Execution is therefore an associated skill by default. New conquistador-leaders will plan and think for your organization, but, above all, will move, execute, implement and conquer.

## Recruitment briefing

Our organization is doing well. A series
of recent acquisitions have expanded
our geographical presence. We have
grown every year. We have remained
loyal to our core business, but we have
lost the sense of conquest that our
founders had.

This may surprise those who follow our
quarterly press releases describing yet
another 'set of met expectations'.

We are now looking for new leaders at
all levels who can explore new
territories and bring back the sense of
quest, adventure and excitement.

Our Strategic Decision number one is to
make curiosity and inquiry our key
competencies.

Our organization is making the numbers
and Wall Street and the City love our
spot-on achievement of predicted EPS.

We are masters of Terra Cognita and we now want to bring the Incognita to the party.

Our Procurement Department is busy trying to provide helmets and spears.

'Been-there-done-that' people need not apply.

## Profile:

- Inquisitorial minds
- Curiosity
- Quest mode
- Spirit of conquest
- Possibly, but not necessarily, ship arsonists
- Cartographers
- Explorers
- Need to show that discovery is a turn-on, versus 'business as usual' (as we've already got that)
- Adventurers

# In the meantime in the office

- Organize a Convention for wild strategies and improbable business plans. Give some prizes and review one top ten finalist every week
- For each wild exploration, find people who can play the role of critic and others to play the role of supporters (i.e. people who are determined to justify the strategy, the expenditure and the business plan)
- Explore dismissed strategies again
- Buy helmets and spears

new leaders wanted: now hiring!

# [ TWELVE ]

## Talki-Walkers

new leaders wanted: now hiring!

# Talki-Walkers

## Walk the talk, the video and the audio

Talki-Walkers are people who take the idea of 'walking the talk' very seriously. They are clearly focused on - if not obsessed with - the thought that whatever they say as leaders (whatever they promise, promote, declare (un)acceptable, etc.), they must show it in practice. An old consultant friend of mine used to say that organizations are full of disconnects between the video and the audio, like those TV-mishaps where the audio in the background and the images do not match. I believe that this is an important leadership problem seen in many organizations.

# walk

Old English. *wealcan* 'to toss, roll', and *wealcian* 'to roll up, curl, muffle up', 'to turn, bend, twist, roll'.

# talk

Related to Medieval English. *tale* 'story'. Also 'to talk, chatter, whisper'.

# trust

From Old Norwegian. *traust* 'help, confidence'. From German. *Trost* 'comfort, consolation, and fidelity'. Related to Old English *treowian* 'to believe'.

The organizational video (the actions we see, what is happening) do not match the organizational audio (what has been said, promised, etc.)

Although everybody should be a Talki-Walker, a synchronous combination of saying and doing make the new leaders of this kind particularly visible and noticeable. The most visible element of their leadership is action following language.

In *The Leader with Seven Faces* (meetingminds, 2006), I propose seven aspects of leadership that should be connected. Most leaders do not exhibit more than one or two and these are the ones that become equivalent to their leadership, the ones that define them. For example, some leaders are very verbal. Language and communication are the face of their leadership. But perhaps their actions are just less visible. In other words, they are best known for what they say. One may guess what they value, but perhaps little is known about what they do. There are many combinations of these seven 'faces', which in summary are:

- What leaders say: the provision of meaning and intention and the language leaders use
- Where leaders go: how they create destinations or journeys or both, and how they become cartographers of the organization
- What leaders build: the architects of space and time, of 'homes' and of legacies

- What leaders care about: the question of values, the use of alibis as 'the system' and what they consider non-negotiable
- How leaders do things: what drives them, styles of leadership and the kind of 'structures' they provide
- What leaders 'are': not 'who', but 'what' they are. The questions of identity, awareness and responsibilities
- What leaders actually do: role modelling, leading change and connecting and practicing the seven faces

When looking at the graph on p. 212, Talki-Walkers always start reading the circle of 'what leaders do'. They usually make the point that this is what really matters, or in stronger words: 'the *only* thing that matters'.

I personally think that other things matter as well. In fact, everything else in my seven faces model matters. But I am sympathetic to the bias. There is little question that organizations are desperate for a good bunch of Talki-Walkers, totally predisposed towards the role modelling aspects of leadership and the consistency between what they say and do. You need those people. They are perfect in three incredibly important areas:

## 1. They build trust big time

Trust is a precious fuel, a consequence of how we defend our vulnerability (I trust you, because I'm able to show you my vulnerability and you don't take advantage of it. You make me feel safe.). It keeps the organization going.

It is also very delicate. It takes a while to build and can be eroded or simply eliminated in one day. The single most powerful driver of trust erosion is breaking promises (or people realizing that what they see in practice is inconsistent with what they heard). Trust professes the most 'unfair' un-linearity of all: small breaches of trust have the power of extrapolation, generalization and of triggering total defence: "*If you have failed me on this one, you'll do it again.*"

Talki-Walkers are reinforcing trust all the time because their primary driver is to behave in a way that shows consistency with the audio. Many Talki-Walkers I know do this in a rather unconscious way.

## 2. They are powerful role models

The power of imitation and/or social copying is enormous. Although one could role model via language, expressions, declaration of values, etc., there is nothing more powerful than overt, observable behaviours. Most of these powerful behaviours are silent. By that I mean that they are not announced and heralded; they happen naturally, not through spin. Good Talki-Walkers are busier with the doing than with the talking. They are walkers first and only then talkers.

Adapted from *The Leader with Seven Faces*
(meetingminds, 2006)

# 3. They practice behavioural translation

Our language is full of things that we call values, beliefs, mindsets, attitudes, etc. We can have good conversations within that vocabulary, but these may happen under the false assumption that we all agree on their specific meaning. Only behaviours are observable and unequivocal. There is no such a thing as honesty, at least not in the same way that there is grey hair or a deep voice. There are behaviours that when exhibited we agree to call honest. From there we then infer and create 'honesty' as a value-concept. The problem with mindsets, attitudes, values, etc. is that they are not operational. We can't do much with them unless we translate those values and beliefs into observable behaviours.

If that's the case, Talki-Walkers have a prime advantage, because that translation into behaviours is the 'raison d'être' of their own identity. They allow us to use the non-behavioural, non-operational language because they give us the comfort of an immediate behavioural translation. If a Talki-Walker promises you honesty, you'll immediately see honesty in action. They prefer to talk less and do more.

The new leader species of Talki-Walkers is precious because of this combined package of (1) trust building, (2) immediate role modelling and (3) behavioural translations. By definition, they connect 'what leaders do' with the other six faces. Because of that, they usually represent a 'rounded' kind of leader.

# Recruitment briefing

We are looking for role models, not glamour-manager models, as we are not a modelling agency but a successful corporation.

In the past, we have been very good at proclaiming our intentions and less good at showing that we meant them. We have had one or two issues with trust.

We are looking for new leaders with a special interest in behaviours that can be imitated, copied or role modelled. We want to practice an active policy of 'by their fruits you shall know them' or 'you will recognize them through their actions'.

We are talking about 'walking the talk', big time. We thought we had that competency, but we just found out that (1) we had a lot of talking and not much walking and (2) where we had both, they didn't match up.

## Profile:

- Behaviours as main interest
- Conscious of the fragility of trust
- Visible actions, including heroic if needed
- Keeps promises
- Action-man first; language part of the package

## In the meantime in the office

- Review all the promises made in the last year and see what's in and what's out
- Find people who walked that talk and describe the situations
- Infect the organization with those stories
- Evaluate your trust capital and find out how much of it has been eroded by some people not walking the talk
- Establish a 'Hall of Fame of Disconnects' where you expose all things and aspects of your organization's life where people have said A and done B. Give prizes for the discovery of these disconnects

# [ Summing up ]

## Moving east

new leaders wanted: now hiring!

# Moving east

The model of the 12 'new kinds of people'
described in this book has directional intentions. It is not
about abandoning the old set of skills, but about recognizing
that pretty much everybody else has the same set. It is hard
to accept and sometimes harsh, but, let's face it, there is a
'me-too' pool and a pool of differentiation and innovation.
The 'me-too' pool doesn't contain bad things. It is exactly
what it says on the tin: 'me-too'.

As usual, the real questions are leadership ones:
how far east are you prepared to go in the summary graph
(on page 221)? What will you have to do to travel east, to
the right hand column, to the differentiated territory? What
kind of leadership team will drive the journey? What sort of

HR policy? What can you do if you are a manager, a divisional head, a team leader or a CEO with different degrees of power and influence?

Don't dismiss the East too soon! At least have a debate about the book after you've read it, individually or as a group. But most of all: keep moving, because it may perhaps not be too late.

| 'ME-TOO' POOL | DIFFERENTIATION AND INNOVATION |
|---|---|
| *Traditional skill set and/or processes that served well in the past and that today are the baseline or a 'pass'* | *New skill set/kinds of people needed to take the organization out of the 'me-too' space towards differentiation and innovation* |

| 'ME-TOO' POOL | DIFFERENTIATION AND INNOVATION |
|---|---|
| • Analytical skills | • Synthesis skills. Integrators. Sense makers |
| • Information/Knowledge Management | • Signal spotters (differentiating signal and noise). Extracting meaning |
| • Time Management | • Space and time creators and protectors |
| • Left brain, orderly management and universal rationality | • Right brain, creative, managing irrationality |
| • Human Resources. People as assets. | • HCIF Management. People as investors |
| • Vertical, unit, divisional, section management. Top down alignment | • Horizontal gluers and binders ('lead(brok)ers') |
| • Teamwork, good team workers. Teamocracy | • Net-workers, relationship builders. Riders of networks. Networkracy |
| • Organization chart management. Clear, orderly boundaries | • Chaordics. Ambiguity management. Acrobats |
| • Best Practices | • Disruptive practices, disruptors |
| • Project and Programme Management | • Backstage/Butterfly Management. Distributed leadership |
| • Strategy Process with 'tyranny of the or' | • Cartographers, explorers, conquistadores |
| • Talk, declaration, missions, followed by actions | • Actions, followed by talk, declarations and missions |

**221**

new leaders wanted: now hiring!

# [ EPILOGUE ]

# Mapping your organization's DNA

new leaders wanted: now hiring!

# Mapping your organization's DNA

This is a totally unscientific, observation-based classification of people, coming from my own organizational consulting practice. I don't claim to have done the research: no 500 CEO interviews, no 2,000 manager questionnaires. The categories that follow have more to do with people's mental programmes than with personalities. They are non-judgmental, neither good nor bad. Good people and difficult people are present throughout. IQ does not correlate with any of them either. It is a polarized variation on the classification that tends to read: you are either one or the other. This is inevitably artificial. Many people may fall in between the extremes or may mix traits, but the dominance of a particular mental programme is what matters. And the compound dominance in your organization is a good snap shot of its behavioural DNA.

We have all been programmed in a particular way by our genes, education and experiences. We carry those mental programmes with us when we get together in 'the organization'. Understanding the diversity in this programming is the first step to functioning socially and, for us, to doing business. The business plot of everyday life needs to be understood through the mental programmes of the characters (people in the organization) and the mental and behavioural framework of the organization (culture).

(Here's the deal: next time you are frustrated and angry because of the incomprehensible behaviour of team-mates or your boss, take a deep breath and try to think about how the perpetrator may have been programmed. It may perhaps help you to understand or perhaps give you an alternative way to respond, attack, change direction or adapt!)

I'd like you to read this epilogue and use it in a slightly light-hearted way. Allow yourself some time to mentally wander around your organization (like looking down from a helicopter) to try and make a judgement about what is dominant from these categories. Your organization (the one you lead, work in and belong to) or any other organization you want to 'test', is bound to host a variety of people, i.e. a variety of behaviours and mental programming. It is important to have a sense of this behavioural DNA and, in particular, to see which traits are dominant and which are missing.

I am asking you to *make a judgement* whilst you read and wander, so that you know a bit better 'how much' of those '12 kinds of people' you need to seek. Think about the principal language in the organization, the predominant people, the patterns that tend to appear in hiring practices…. It is not mathematics, but your judgement that counts. The categories are bimodal by nature and therefore a caricature. But you must have a sense of where in the spectrum of each of the 12 dimensions your organization is better represented. Use the charts at the end of this chapter to rank your assessment.

Incidentally, these 12 dimensions do not correlate one by one with the 12 kinds of people. I have mixed up the categories on purpose, so that you are not tempted to follow the order of the chapters of the book.

## 1. Sequence:

There are 'parallel people' and 'sequential people'. Parallel people are able to work (mentally and physically) on several tracks at the same time. They are jumpers. They navigate very well from one thing to another, by switching between ideas and tasks. They have no problem with 'unfinished' issues to be finished later on. Sequential people, however, need to go from A to B first, and from B to C afterwards. Don't interrupt them in their sequence or dare to ask what's going to happen with D. In their minds, this is a stupid question - they are still solving B. Their view of the parallel people is that they are messy and unmethodical, prone to sloppiness. Parallel people think that the sequential ones are rigid and 'one-ball jugglers', often at the expense of everybody else. Which one is dominant in your organization? Use the chart to mark your thoughts.

## 2. Uncertainty:

There are 'data (facts)-driven' people and 'strategy (goal)-driven' people. Data-driven people dislike uncertainty. For them, decisions need to be based on solid research or facts. Guessing, 'what if' or speculating is considered a waste of time. Goal-driven people 'see' the future and work backwards. They have no problem with the lack of current data; they love scenarios and possibilities. Whilst they agree that facts and data are needed, they often 'can't wait'. They need to imagine the future and play with choices. They think that data-driven people lack imagination. Beware: it may be fashionable or even politically correct to declare that the entire organization is strategy-driven. After all, you have a strategy and people follow. The distinction here is whether the focus of attention is first strategy/goals or data. I know you are going to say that you need both, but look around and decide where your people spend most of the time. Then use the chart to note your findings.

# 3. Channels:

People have preferred sensors and channels to see, understand and communicate with the world. There are verbal people, visual people and/or people who like things written down. Entire corporate cultures are shaped by sensor and channel preferences. There are voice mail, email, fax and telephone cultures. You need to understand those preferences and adjust your channels; otherwise you'll need to be prepared for surprises. A one-slide bubble chart won't do it for the boss expecting a full report. For other people, nothing less than a face-to-face or a personal call is expected – don't send them 'the slides'. Think of your organization from that helicopter view and make a judgement as to what the dominance is. I know you have all of them, but, again, where are your colleagues spending their time now? Have a go and use the chart to mark your thoughts.

# 4. Units:

'Atomic people' dissect the elephant (the problem) into pieces and deal with legs, tails and ears separately. 'Molecular people' see an elephant when all they see is a combination of body parts. Atomic people thrive in an analytical environment (and should have no problems answering job ads – as we said before, everybody seems to ask for analytic skills!), whilst molecular people are synthetic by programming, the kind of people usually referred to as having a 'helicopter view' of things. Molecular people often refer to the others as 'lost in the detail'. Atomic people see the others as 'not detailed enough', meaning not to be trusted if you need a job done well! I know these are caricatures, but what do you think of your organization? Use the chart.

## 5. Decisions:

'Open-decision people' are happy to park issues and postpone or defer an outcome; literally leaving the decision open. 'Closed-decision people' are always desperate to reach a resolution and close the topic, sometimes at any cost. They think open-decision people are always paralyzed and have poor leadership qualities (making decisions and leadership are synonymous to them). If you are a closed-decision person and want to force a resolution in an environment (team, customer group) that needs more time to reflect, you may get frustrated unnecessarily. Or, if you are about to make a deal with a 'closed-decision' person (or organization), and you function with the opposite mental programme, you may misread them as too eager or desperate. They just may not have the concept of 'reviewing it again tomorrow' in their mental programming. Again, use the chart to note down how this fits within your organization.

## 6. Propositions:

Some people focus on a question, proposal or statement first and then develop the idea and the arguments further. I call them 'the journalists'. Others do exactly the opposite. I call them 'the lawyers'. Consider these two memos:

A. *"This is to request the hiring of a new manager. The situation in the office has become unbearable; we have such and such project and these deadlines, etc..."* (Then development of the ideas and reasons follow over one or two pages).

B. *"We have become inundated by projects and are under a lot of pressure to meet deadlines.* (Then, two or three pages of more details, reasons and explanations follow) *That is why I am requesting a new manager."*

In A the request is upfront; in B it comes three pages later. A is journalistic. The theory in journalism about the human attention span says that 'the message' must be in the first paragraph. However, many legal documents - from petitions to court rulings - follow the style of B: "*considering such and such* (one page), *having heard N and N* (one page), *and taking into account X and Y, we declare that* (the statement, at the end)". Many people think that the sharpness of the 'journalistic' model A means a well-organized mind, while model B indicates verbose and disorganized people. This is not how the B-stylists see themselves! They think they are more logical in their flow of thought! What's the predominant style in your organization? Have a go and mark the chart.

## 7. Simplicity:

This has to do with the ability of people to create and convey simple messages, whether they come from a simple or complex topic. Some scientific writers have this ability, explaining complex science in ways that even lay people can understand. Other people simply can't do that. In some business cultures, the norm and expectations are '1,2,3', 'one-page summary, 'in three bullet points' and 'the net-net'. Don't go to them with an intricate elaboration based on Chaos and Complexity Theory. Paul Valéry said: "*Everything that is simple is wrong; everything that is not is unusable*". That dilemma is still looking for a solution in business life today. What's representative of your organization? Have a go and rate it in the chart.

## 8. Inclusiveness:

Some people ask for opinions and go around the table (or the company) for recommendations, before (perhaps) finally making a decision. They are 'constituency people' - sensitive to the inclusion of as many players as possible. Others are 'ad hoc people' - they will ask you for an opinion or a recommendation only if you are key to the topic; otherwise, they would genuinely consider it a waste of time. At one end of the spectrum, entire organizations suffer from Over-Inclusiveness Syndrome: everybody must be (or wants to be) involved in everything. At the other end sit organizations with no collective soul and a pretty good organization chart to make sure that one knows whom not to ask in the chain of command. If you are a newly appointed 'ad hoc' boss in a 'constituency' organization, you will soon earn (most likely unfairly) the label of autocrat. Now, what do you think is predominantly going on in your organization? Make a judgement and mark the chart.

## 9. Authority:

Cultures have been classified according to their attitudes towards authority. What applies to cultures applies to individuals as well. 'Status people' will follow hierarchy-based authority. 'Wisdom people' regard authority as something that somebody earns (moral, knowledge, etc.). Always check this out before embarking on any new partnership! For clues, watch the body language around the negotiating table. Ten pairs of eyes looking in one direction? He's the man. I know that you may be prone to respond that you have both wisdom and status. That is probably true and I am not saying that they are mutually exclusive. But once again I'd like you to make a judgement as if you were looking down from a helicopter.

## 10. Project:

There are 'doing what people' (task-oriented) and 'doing how people' (process-oriented). The former have an eye on the destination; they love milestones, distinct tasks with clear desirable outcomes and they are often simply referred to as 'doers'. For them, *how* to get there is less relevant. Indeed, they may get there at any cost. The 'doing how people' focus on the journey and the way things are done matters a lot. I know you probably have both, but what is the predominant language and where do your people spend most of their time? Make a judgment and rate the scale.

## 11. Time:

There are 'past', 'present' and 'future' people. They differ in their reference to the world. To anchor everything in the past with somebody working in next-century time, leads to a dialogue that falls on deaf ears. Those better equipped with 'past-time' mental programmes choose professions accordingly: archaeologists, historians or psychoanalysts. They may not be the best to invent the Third-Generation Internet, but you don't want Bill Gates as psychotherapist either. Short-termism in current business life has led to a new breed of 'present time' managers who count time in 'quarters'. Where is your organization in this dimension? When in doubt, think about where you spend most of your time.

## 12. Options:

There are people who tend to follow one single, logical, linear thinking path, probably the one that makes more sense to them, and they are happy with the outcome. In chapter four, I called them 'therefore people'. They sound like this: *"we have done A, have taken into consideration all the risks and listened to all, therefore we must choose X"*. It is solid and reassuring. Other people can't stick to one linear track, even if that track is very reasonable. I call them 'however people'. They sound like this: *"We have done A, explored B, and we think we should do X. However, we could also do Y and Z"*. Each of them has a tremendous ability to irritate the other. The former are seen as rigid or, more benevolently, 'determined' by the latter, who in turn are seen as 'unclear' and indecisive by the 'therefore people'. What's the predominant side in your organization? What would I see most if I spent some time with you and your people? Make a judgement and rate the scale.

## SEQUENCE

Parallel          Sequential

—— 3 — 2 – 1 – 0 — 1 — 2 — 3 —

| Most people | Some people | Very few | No idea | Very few | Some people | Most people |

## UNCERTAINTY

Strategy & goal driven       Data driven

—— 3 — 2 – 1 – 0 — 1 — 2 — 3 —

| Most people | Some people | Very few | No idea | Very few | Some people | Most people |

## CHANNELS

Visual and face to face       Verbal and Written (email)

— 3 — 2 – 1 – 0 — 1 — 2 — 3 —

| Most people | Some people | Very few | No idea | Very few | Some people | Most people |

## UNITS

Molecular (elephants)       Atomic (legs, ears and tusks)

— 3 — 2 – 1 – 0 — 1 — 2 — 3 —

| Most people | Some people | Very few | No idea | Very few | Some people | Most people |

**236** |

## DECISIONS

Open and/or parked                     Close asap

— 3 — 2 – 1 – 0 – 1 — 2 — 3 —

| Most people | Some people | Very few | No idea | Very few | Some people | Most people |

## PROPOSITIONS

Journalist                             Lawyer

— 3 — 2 – 1 – 0 – 1 — 2 — 3 —

| Most people | Some people | Very few | No idea | Very few | Some people | Most people |

## SIMPLICITY

Complexity                             Complexity
Explained                              Reduced
(stories)                              (bullet points)

— 3 — 2 – 1 – 0 – 1 — 2 — 3 —

| Most people | Some people | Very few | No idea | Very few | Some people | Most people |

## INCLUSIVENESS

Constituency                           Ad hoc

— 3 — 2 – 1 – 0 – 1 — 2 — 3 —

| Most people | Some people | Very few | No idea | Very few | Some people | Most people |

## AUTHORITY

Wisdom                                          Status

—— 3 — 2 – 1 – 0 – 1 — 2 — 3 ——

| Most people | Some people | Very few | No idea | Very few | Some people | Most people |

## PROJECT

Doing how                                    Doing what

—— 3 — 2 – 1 – 0 – 1 — 2 — 3 ——

| Most people | Some people | Very few | No idea | Very few | Some people | Most people |

## TIME

Future                              Present & Past

—— 3 — 2 – 1 – 0 – 1 — 2 — 3 ——

| Most people | Some people | Very few | No idea | Very few | Some people | Most people |

## OPTIONS

However                                    Therefore

—— 3 — 2 — 1 – 0 — 1 — 2 — 3 ——

| Most people | Some people | Very few | No idea | Very few | Some people | Most people |

## SCORES AND INTERPRETATION

Add up all the numbers on each side. What matters is the relative ratio between the two columns.

- Total Left hand column    =        points
- Total Right hand column   =        points
- Grand total of both columns =        points

[Total Left side x 100] / Grand Total = Score A

[Total Right side x 100] / Grand Total = Score B

If the scores are very similar, you have a rather balanced organizational DNA in terms of 'new kinds of people' vs. the more conventional set of skills and competencies. This is good news, but you still need to identify your 'new kinds of people' inside the organization and transform them even more into participants and protagonists.

When score B is much higher than score A, that means you should start recruiting now and find, seduce, hire and create a job for as many of the 12 kinds of people as you can. Don't despair. Your organization is not bad, dysfunctional or necessarily in trouble. Actually, it is pretty normal… and that's the problem!

When the opposite is true, you have hit the jackpot and your organization is well populated by 'new kinds of people'. Your mission: retention. Also, ask yourself how you got there, so that you can learn from your own success.

# About the author

**Leandro Herrero** practiced as a psychiatrist for more than fifteen years before taking up senior management positions in several leading global companies, both in Europe and the US.

He is founder and CEO of The Chalfont Project Ltd, an international consulting firm of organizational architects. Taking advantage of his behavioural sciences background – coupled with his hands-on business experience – he works with organizations of many kinds on structural and behavioural change, leadership and human collaboration.

Other than his medical and psychiatric qualifications, he holds an MBA and is Fellow of the Chartered Management Institute and the Institute of Directors (UK). He is also a member of the Advisory Board at the Operational Research Department (part of the new Department of Management) at the London School of Economics.

He has published several books, among which *The Leader with Seven Faces* and *Viral Change*.

# \<meetingminds\>

## Viral Change:
### The alternative to slow, painful and unsuccessful management of change in organizations
By Leandro Herrero

Many 'Change Management' initiatives end in fiasco, because they only focus on processes and systems. But there is no change, unless the change is behavioural.

*Viral Change* is THE manager's handbook on how to create sustainable and long-lasting change in organizations.

The author says: "*If change is needed, the traditional 'change management models' may not be the most effective vehicle. Most of those change management systems fail because they do not deliver behavioural change in the individuals. Viral Change is different... and it works*!"

You can listen to the author talk about *Viral Change* at **www.meetingminds.com**, where you can also read the introduction and more info on the book.

*Viral Change* is available from Amazon, Barnes and Noble, Blackwell, WH Smith, Borders, Books Etc. and many other online bookshops, as well as from www.meetingminds.com

## <u>Special offer:</u> email **sales@meetingminds.com**
mentioning code 'NEWL' and you can buy *Viral Change* at £12.95/$19.45 US (+ shipping), saving 35%!

# \<meetingminds\>

## The Leader with Seven Faces:
### Finding your own ways of practicing leadership in today's organization
By Leandro Herrero

After all the books written about leadership, you'd think we know a thing or two about leadership. However, nothing seems to be further from the truth.

*The Leader with Seven Faces* provides a novel approach to leadership where the questions to ask (about what leaders say, where they go, what they build, care about, do, how they do it and 'what' they are) take priority over producing 'universal answers'.

For anybody interested in leadership of organizations... and in seeing things through a new pair of glasses.

*The Leader with Seven Faces* is available from Amazon, Barnes and Noble, Blackwell, WH Smith, Borders, Books Etc. and many other online bookshops, as well as from www.meetingminds.com

**Special offer:** email **sales@meetingminds.com** mentioning code 'NEWL' and you can buy *The Leader with Seven Faces* at £12.95/$19.45 (+ shipping), saving 35%!

# \<meetingminds\>

**To order extra copies of New Leaders Wanted,** visit our website at www.meetingminds.com. It is also available from Amazon, Barnes and Noble, Blackwell, WH Smith, Borders, Books Etc. and many other online bookshops. For bulk orders, please contact us directly for more information on discounts and shipping costs.

**Customized editions:** These are special editions created for a particular audience such as a specific **company or organization**. The core materials of the book are maintained, but relevant company-specific resources - such as in-house case studies or tool-kits – are added. A **special foreword** or tailored introduction - written either by the author or by your company's leadership - may be added as well. The book cover could also be adapted. Using modern printing technology, we can supply virtually any number of copies, from small runs to bulk production. If you are interested, please contact us.

**Continue the conversation:** There are many ways you can engage the author, from speaking opportunities to consulting services facilitating a change process and/or enabling your internal resources to drive change and leadership. Details can be obtained via **www.thechalfontproject.com**, through which you can also contact the author.

### \<meetingminds\>
PO Box 1192, HP9 1YQ, United Kingdom
Tel. +44 (0)208 123 8910 - **www.meetingminds.com**
info@meetingminds.com

.

# INDEX

CPSIA information can be obtained
at www.ICGtesting.com
Printed in the USA
LVOW08s0029080317
526486LV00001B/10/P